Reel Mediation

A DISPUTE RESOLUTION JOURNEY THROUGH FILM

Helen Leah Lightstone

 FriesenPress

One Printers Way
Altona, MB R0G 0B0
Canada

www.friesenpress.com

ISBN
978-1-03-913261-0 (Hardcover)
978-1-03-913260-3 (Paperback)
978-1-03-913262-7 (eBook)

1. LAW, ALTERNATIVE DISPUTE RESOLUTION

Distributed to the trade by The Ingram Book Company

WITH SPECIAL THANKS TO

Brian Empson, Moishe Fogel, Heather and Peter Gilies,
Michael Gulycz, Margret Husistein, Gail Kaplansky,
Michael Lamothe, Cookie Pearl and Esme Lightstone,
Mort Lightstone, Sarah Lightstone, Leslie MacLeod,
Lee-Anne Moore, Jon Thibert, Dr.Bob Watson, B.SC.,
DVM., and Rob Wilson and Tracy Husistein-Wilson

Table of Contents

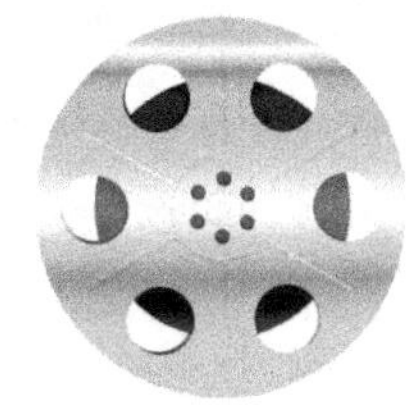

DEDICATION

There is a Persian proverb that suggests "water will eventually find its path." Through my journey, there is not a truer statement to help me understand why I am where I am today.

Thank you so much to all those who walked with me during my dispute resolution journey. They include Stacey Alderwick, The Honourable Todd Archibald, Colm Brannigan, Peter Bruer, Blaine Donais, Gary Furlong, Sir Marston Gibson, Frank Gomberg, Hilary Linton, Frank McLean, Cinnie Noble, Michelle Sauvé and Regina Thompson. You are who I aspire to be when I grow up. I would like to thank Michael (Mike) Gulycz who was my first Alternative Dispute Resolution (ADR) instructor during my paralegal studies at Seneca College. One day, I went back to Mike and thanked him for everything he taught me during the ADR classes, and he said to me; "Don't thank me, thank the person you look at in the mirror every day." To this day, I believe he is wrong.

Finally, I would love to thank all my college and Lightstone Academy for Conflict Resolution students, who have also taught me a great deal. Robert Heinlein suggests:

"When one teaches, two learn." I could not agree more with Robert Heinlein. So, I thank you, my students, for having me on this journey with you, and I look forward to what you will accomplish.

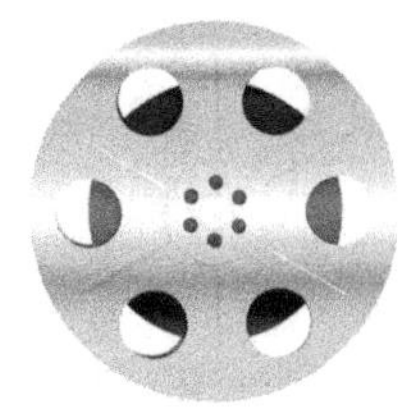

INTRODUCTION

For over 125 years, we have been captivated by the art of film, starting with the first soundless motion picture film in 1927, to the most advanced computer-generated images and the greatest visual and special effects to date. Film has the capacity to take us back in time, bring us to new worlds, and take us on a roller-coaster of emotions. "Love means never having to say you're sorry"[1] left audiences weeping during Love Story,[2] and in 1960, this line, "Norman Bates's mother has been dead and buried in Greenlawn Cemetery for the past ten years,"[3] chilled the cinematic viewers of Alfred Hitchcock's Psycho.[4] Historic influences, the power of love, the fluid impact of culture, and the multi-layered impact of politics provided the audience an immersive sensory experience and an opportunity to understand concepts they had never imagined, and, as such, film has the overwhelming ability to educate the masses, one person at a time.

The purpose of this Major Research Paper (MRP) is to question whether film contributes to the pedagogy of dispute resolution. In order to provide a logical flow, the MRP will follow the LL.M., (Dispute Resolution) at Osgoode at York University and will include, in chronological order: 1) Introduction to Dispute Resolution;[5] 2) Theory and Practice of Dispute Resolution;[6]

---

1   iTunes, "Love Story" (4 March 2017), at 00h:59m:01s

2   iTunes, "Love Story" (4 March 2017), The movie may be accessed through: http://www.apple.com/ca/itunes/

3   iTunes, "Psycho" (4 March 2017), at 01h:23:53s

4   iTunes, "Psycho" (4 March 2017), The movie may be accessed through: http://www.apple.com/ca/itunes/

5   Paul Emond, Adjunct Professor Leslie H. Macleod, *Coursepack: Introduction to Dispute Resolution* (Faculty of Law, Osgoode Hall Law School, at York University, Fall 2015) at 1.

6   Leslie H. Macleod, *Coursepack: The Theory and Practice of Dispute Resolution*

Process Design;[7] 4) Advanced Mediation;[8] and 5) Culture, Diversity, and Power.[9]

• • •

In order to highlight the dispute resolution program, several films have been used to demonstrate key components of dispute resolution. The films choices for the MRP include: 1) Introduction to Dispute Resolution[10]will discuss 12 Angry Men,[11] The Tenth Man,[12] and Women in Gold;[13] 2) Theory and Practice of Dispute Resolution[14] will utilize Music from the Big House;[15] 3) Process Design will explore Colonia;[16] 4) Advanced Mediation, War of the Roses;[17] and 5) Culture, Diversity, and Power[18] will speak to Gran Torino[19]

- -

(Faculty of Law, Osgoode Hall Law School, at York University, Fall 2015) at 1.

7   Leslie H. Macleod, *Coursepack: Dispute Analysis and Process Design* (Faculty of Law, Osgoode Hall Law School, at York University, Winter 2016) at 1.

8   Michaela Keet, *Coursepack: Advanced Dispute Resolution* (Faculty of Law, Osgoode Hall Law School, at York University, Summer 2016) at 1.

9   Michelle LeBaron, *Coursepack: Culture Diversity and Power in Dispute Resolution* (Faculty of Law, Osgoode Hall Law School, at York University, Spring 2016) at 1.

10 *Introduction, supra* note 5.

11 *12 Angry Men*, DVD (Beverly Hills, Cal: Twentieth Century Fox Home Entertainment, 2008)

12 *The Tenth Man*, DVD (Metro Goldwyn Mayer, 2005).

13 iTunes, "Woman in Gold" (December 2015). Online: iTunes <C: Users\Owner\Music\iTunes \iTunes\Media\Movies\Woman in Gold(HD).m4>

14 *Theory, supra* note 6

15 *Music From the Big House*, DVD (Caché Film and Television, 2012)

16 Netflix, "Colonia" (November 2015). Online: Netflix <www.netflix.com/search?q=Colonia>. The author of this paper discovered the movie ceased to be available through Netflix as of 14th of July 2020 from Netflix), therefore a hyperlink is not possible.

17 ITunes, "War of the Roses" (December 2016). Online: iTunes < C:\Users\Owner\Music\iTunes\iTunes Media\Movies\The War of the Roses\The War of the Roses (HD).m4>

18 *Culture, supra* note 9.

19 *Gran Torino*, DVD (Warner Bros. Pictures, 2008).

4

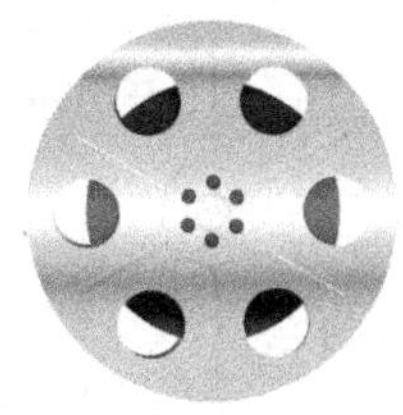

VISUAL LEARNERS

Film, television, and other media are fast becoming venues for learning, as film provides a platform that helps us understand how the world works around us and allows students to look at concepts from different perspectives. The online article, "Teaching with Film,"[20] suggests this is an important tool when 65% of students are visual learners:[21]

• • •

> Visual Today's students are more affected by visual media than ever before [as] an integral part of their lives, students seldom need to be coaxed into watching films, film evokes emotion and provokes stimulating discussion and, students learn best when they are excited.[22]

In order to address what type of student learns better by film, it is necessary to review the different learning styles, as presented by Kolb, Gardener, Bandura, and Pratt. To begin, Kolb created the "Kolb Learning Style Inventory,"[23] a four-quadrant chart that places students in one or several of the following: accommodating, diverging, assimilating, and converging. Students who adapt better to media, such as film, would appeal more to the diverging quadrant, due to a larger focus on the concrete experience of feeling. These students prefer to watch and "use their imagination to figure it out, and are best at viewing concrete situations

---

20 *Teaching with Film.* (n.d.). Retrieved January 2016, from Journeys in Film: https://journeysinfilm.org/why-teach-with-film/

21 *Ibid.*

22 *Ibid.*

23 Mary Giardina, *Coursepack: Teaching and Training Adults, Coursepack* (Faculty of Seneca College Fall 2011) at 2.

at several different viewpoints."[24] The name for this group of students is "diverging."

Educational theorist Howard Gardener created "Multiple Intelligences Theory,"[25] which addresses eight different intelligences, each of us having strengths and weaknesses in each one. However, the intelligence most likely associated with those who would benefit from film is visual/spatial learners and is defined by Gardener as:

> Visual/Spatial intelligence refers to the ability to form and manipulate a mental model. Individuals with strength in this area depend on visual thinking and are very imaginative. People with this kind of intelligence tend to learn most readily from visual presentations such as movies, pictures, videos, and demonstrations using models and props.[26]

However, after reviewing various learning theories, Bandura's "Social Learning Theory" may appeal to most visual learners. Bandura's theory is referred to as modeling or observational learning. His theory suggests that people learn from other people by observing other individuals and/or modeling their behaviour. Observational learning includes four steps: paying attention to learn, retaining the information, reproducing the task, and having a reason or motivation to learn.

While these learning theories are brief, they do provide some insight as to why film might be included in "Universal Design Theories" (UDL). The three main ideas behind UDL are to provide multiple means of presenting the information, provide different ways for the students to demonstrate what they have learned and finally, stimulate interest, thereby providing motivation to learn. UDL is found not only at Durham College Centre for Faculty Enrichment (CAFE)[27] but is embedded in the development of mainstream curriculum all over the world.

According to the "Universal Design for Learning (UDL) Guidelines at Durham College,"[28] the use of film is referenced twice in the third principle as a means to instruct.

---

24 *Teaching, supra* note 23.

25 (Resources, n.d.)

26 *Giardina, supra* note 23.

27 Durham College, "Overview of 3 UDL Principles", online: < https:// durhamcollege.ca/ctl/teaching/planning-to-teach/udl/3-udl-principles/ >.

28 *Ibid.*

Checkpoint 3.3 - Guide information processing, visualization, and manipulation implementation strategies, Provide multiple entry points to a lesson and optional pathways through content (e.g., exploring big ideas through dramatic works, arts and literature, film and media).

Checkpoint 3.4 - Maximize transfer and generalization

Embed new ideas in familiar ideas and contexts (e.g., use of analogy, metaphor, drama, music, film, etc.)[29]

Educational theorist Daniel Pratt suggests in the article "Lights, Camera, Action! The Role of Movies and Video in Classroom Learning (Lights)"[30] that not only do students approach learning differently, but so do faculty. Pratt suggests there are five perspectives teachers consider when considering the delivery of course content, and they include transmission, apprentice, development, nurturing and social reform. These perspectives will be addressed further in the paper to support how film contributes to the pedagogy of teaching.

29 *Ibid.*

30 Pamela Eddy, Daniel Bracken, "Lights, Camera, Action! The Role of Movies and Video in Classroom Learning", (2008) 22 Journal of Faculty Development 2 online: < https://www.questia.com/library/journal/1P3- 1619018211/ lights-camera-action-the-role-of-movies-and-video>. The author of this paper discovered the website ceased to be available, as of December 21st, 2020, therefore a hyperlink is not possible.

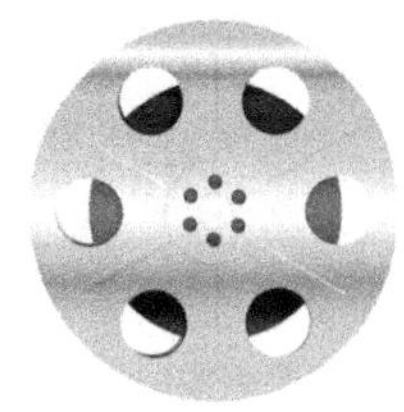

INTRODUCTION TO DISPUTE RESOLUTION[31]

NEGOTIATION, MEDIATION AND ARBITRATION

Three films demonstrate negotiation, mediation, and arbitration and parallel the interest-based, rights-based, and power-based methods of conflict resolution, as confirmed on the "Appropriate Dispute Resolution Continuum."[32] The Tenth Man[33] is a World War Two (WWII) film that addresses what appears to be a very simple interest-based negotiation between the incarcerated Anthony Hopkins (Chavel) and another prisoner, Michel Mangeot. 12 Angry Men,[34] a rights-based film, addresses one particular juror who possesses exceptional active listening skills and neutrality, needed by mediators today. Finally, Woman in Gold[35] exemplifies an arbitration process, as real-life Maria Altmann sues the Austrian government in 2004 over precious artwork owned by her family but appropriated by the power-based Nazis during WWII.

---

31 *Introduction, supra* note 5.

32 Paul Emond, Adjunct Professor Leslie H. Macleod, *Coursepack: Introduction to Dispute Resolution* (Faculty of Law, Osgoode Hall Law School, at York University, Fall 2015) at 5.

33 *Tenth, supra* note 12.

34 *12, supra* note 11.

35 *Woman, supra* note 13.

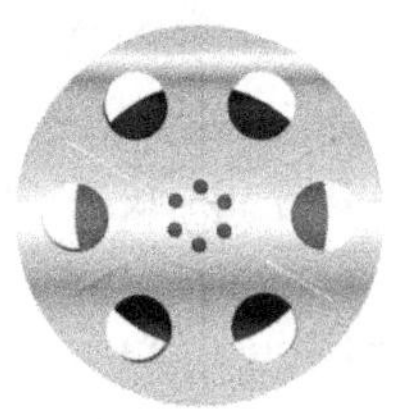

NEGOTIATION

The Tenth Man[36] appeals to visual/spatial learners who depend on visual thinking and are very imaginative. They thrive on complexity and are systems thinkers. In order to appeal to the visual/spatial learner, the perspective teacher would find the transmission perspective useful, as this allows the teacher to stop, pause, and break down content components. For example, this would allow the visual/spatial learner to understand the links required to enter into a negotiation.

Giving visual life to interest-based negotiation in The Tenth Man,[37] set during the occupation of France during WWII, Anthony Hopkins plays the role of Jean-Louis Chavel of St. Jean de Brinac, a successful and wealthy lawyer. One

36   *Tenth, supra* note 12.

37   *Tenth, supra* note 12.

morning, on his way to his office in Paris, Chavel is one of thirty men rounded up by the Nazis and imprisoned for seemingly no reason.

To be made an example of to the citizens of occupied Paris, one in every ten prisoners must be executed, and the guards leave it to the men to choose three doomed souls from amongst them. To accomplish this devastating task, it is decided that thirty pieces of scrap paper will be used, three with an X written on them and twenty-seven without. Jean-Louis Chavel chooses a piece of paper with an X and his fate is sealed; he and two other men will be executed in the morning. While the two men accept their fate, Chavel is desperate to live and pleads to the twenty-nine others whom he shares a cell:

Chavel:	I'll give a hundred thousand francs to anyone, who'll take this? A hundred thousand francs. Please. A hundred thousand. Please. A hundred thousand francs. I'll give a hundred thousand francs, please![38]
Condemned Man 1:	"No one's going to give his life for money he'll never enjoy. It's obvious.[39]

However, he soon discovers a party willing to engage in the negotiation process, much to the surprise of every man in the prison cell, and quickly finds himself in an interest-based negotiation, as described by Julie MacFarlane and her book *Dispute Resolution Readings and Case Studies (Dispute Resolution Readings)*[40]:

> [The art and science of negotiation]… is concerned with situations in which two or more parties recognize the differences of interest and values exist among them and in which they want (or in which one or more are compelled) to see a compromise agreement through negotiation.[41]

In prison, Chavel finds his negotiation partner in fellow inmate Michel Mangeot, a down-and-out single-man with terminal tuberculosis,[42] a sick mother, and a

---

38   *Tenth supra* note 12. At 00h:18m:52s.

39   *Tenth supra* note 12. At 00h:19m:13s.

40   Macfarlane, J. *Dispute Resolution Readings, and Case Studies* (Toronto, ON: Emond Montgomery Publications Limited, 2011).

41   *Ibid.*

42   Although this is not clear in the film, further readings suggest Mangeot was dying from tuberculosis.

sister of marriageable age, all presumably destitute. With the following sentence by Mangeot, an interest-based negotiation commences—"Tell me more, maybe I'll take your offer."[43]—to which Chavel responds, "A hundred thousand francs. My land, my house, everything I've got."[44] While Chavel and Mangeot's underlying interests are straightforward, I want to live versus I want to die, the storyline provides for current negotiation principles.

Following this matter-of-fact exchange, Mangeot and Chavel have now entered into a dependent[45] negotiation in which both parties " …rely on others for what they need; because they need the help, benevolence, or the cooperation of the other, the dependent party must accept and accommodate that provider's whim and idiosyncrasies,"[46] unlike an independent negotiation, which allows for the parties to work without the assistance of others, or an interdependent negotiation, which allows a dovetailing of common goals. As the goals of each party are quite different to each other, it rules out an interdependent and independent negotiation, leaving a dependent negotiation where each party needs something from the other.

In many instances, the negotiation between Chavel and Mangeot is simple; it demonstrates an integrative, win-win solution to a conflict and that they are value creators,[47] or parties to a dispute who are "inventive and cooperative enough to devise an agreement that yields a considerable gain to each party, relative to no-agreement possibilities."[48] Further discussion of value creators suggests that exploring and discussing the underlying interests of the other party "can become the basis for new and creative agreements." [49] While Chavel's interest may simply be to live, Mangeot, knowing that he is ill, wants his mother and sister taken care of and to die a rich man. Both Chavel and Mangeot, according to Macfarlane,[50] negotiate for one of five basic needs—for Mangeot, economic wellbeing, and for Chavel, control of over one's life.

---

43   *Tenth supra* note 12. At 00h:19m:34s.

44   *Tenth supra* note 12. At 00h:19m:46s.

45   *Dispute Resolution Readings, supra* Note 40 at 109

46   *Ibid.*

47   *Dispute Resolution Readings, supra* note 40 at 124.

48   *Ibid.*

49   *Dispute Resolution Readings, supra* note 40 at 130.

50   *Dispute Resolution Readings, supra* note 40 at 135.

Chavel:	You'll take my place?
Michel Mangeot:	I'll take your place.
Prisoner 1:	What use is his money when you're dead?
Michel Mangeot:	I have a mother and a sister; I can make a will.
Condemned Man 1:	I don't like this. We can't buy our lives, why should he?
Prisoner 2:	If you've got money, you can do what you like. Buy another man's life? Why not?!
Prisoner 3:	It's not fair.
Michel Mangeot:	Why isn't it fair to let me do what I want? I'm going to die a rich man. Anyone who thinks it isn't fair can rot in hell. (Coughs) [To Mangeot:] Come here, sit down.[51]

Interesting also, both Chavel and Mangeot quickly establish their bargaining range. A bargaining range is the distance between their aspiration level and their reservation price. In order to establish this range, they needed to consider the following: first, their aspiration level,[52] or their ideal result—Chavel wants to live and Mangeot want to die; next is their negotiating goal,[53] better defined as what each party would be happy to settle for. In both instances, their negotiating goal echoes their aspiration level and finally their reservation price,[54], or their walk-away point. From Chavel's perspective, his only walk-away point would be a change of heart from Mangeot, and Mangeot's walk -way point would be anything less than everything from Chavel. The bargaining range between Chavel and Mangeot is what Dispute Resolution[55] refers to as a viable option, where a possible resolution suggests:

… That agreement is more likely and more rapid the larger the bargaining range, presumably because there are more viable options. The only exception to this generalization would appear to be the unusual circumstance where each party knows the other's limit. In this case, it may appear to have a single viable option rather than several, because this option is likely to become a prominent solution.[56]

---

51 *Tenth, supra* note 12. At 00h:20m:12s.

52 *Dispute Resolution Readings, supra* note 40 at 121.

53 *Ibid.*

54 *Ibid.*

55 *Dispute Resolution Readings, supra* note 40 at 118.

56 *Ibid.*

The above statement seems to ring true for the outcome of this negotiation; each party knows the other's limits, and a single viable option is created and there is no room for a negotiation goal.

A telling line from Prisoner 2 introduces the audience to a key concept in these negotiations—that of power—and it would be remiss to ignore it: "If you've got money you can do what you like. Buy another man's life? Why not?!"[57]

Even though Mangeot appears to be at a disadvantage and unlikely to agree to the terms Chavel is offering, he may hold more power than Chavel believes. Mangeot's power would be referred to as a resource power "…based on some resource [he] has, such as time,"[58] or in this instance, his greatest resource: his own life. Similarly, Chavel holds a great deal of financial power, also a resource power, as he has the ability to offer money in exchange for his life. It is possible that had he not had the finances that he did, the negotiation would never have taken place, and his premature death would have been met before a firing squad. Chavel nor Mangeot ever took for granted the power the other party had, and while Mangeot could have believed that Chavel was too powerful to refuse, he understood the power that he brought to the table. Due to their dependent relationship, the two men were able to achieve an integrative negotiation that met both of their needs.

The Tenth Man[59] appeals to visual/spatial learners who depend on visual thinking, are very imaginative, thrive on complexity and are systems thinkers. The perspective teacher allows the student to stop, pause, and break down content components to enter into a negotiation. As such, films like The Tenth Man[60] offer an opportunity to engage visual learners and provide an opportunity similar to experiential learning, thereby fostering and expanding upon the instructor's toolkit for lessons.

---

57 *Tenth, supra* note 12. At 00h:20m:08s.

58 Ewert, C. et al, *Choices in Approaching Conflict: Understanding the Practice of Alternative Dispute Resolution* (Toronto, ON: Emond Montgomery Publications Limited, 2010).

59 *Tenth, supra* note 12.

60 *Tenth supra* note 12.

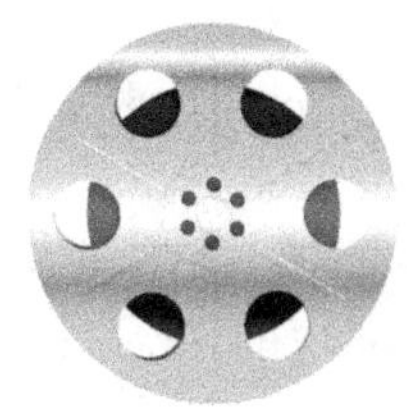

MEDIATION

12 Angry Men[61] is the story of a young man on trial for the murder of his father. It is a film used in law schools around the world to address legal concepts such as reasonable doubt, evidence, and unanimous verdicts. As it relates to the pedagogy of dispute resolution, this is an influential film today, as it exemplifies qualities relevant to dispute resolution, such as the role of a mediator, as best illustrated by Henry Fonda is Juror Eight, a rights-based process, and the use of active listening skills.[62] This film appeals to those who subscribe to Pratt's accommodator style—who, after viewing a film, would demonstrate the skill set of an active listener in a forthcoming exercise and/or follow-up discussion. This would appeal to the apprentice perspective of instruction, as it allows the student to

61   *12, supra* Note 11.

62   Helen Lightstone, "12 Angry Men: Themes, Conflict Theory and Mediators" (2016) 3.

reproduce the skillset demonstrated in the film.

The first images of the courtroom establish an adversarial rights-based process where we understand that the lawyers for the defence and the prosecution have been heard, and the evidence and testimony have been given. Shortly after, the judge instructs the jury that since they have listened to the evidence, they are to separate the "facts from the fancy"[63] and come to a unanimous decision. At the end of the jury deliberations, if the jurors find the accused guilty, the court will have no mercy, and the young man will be executed. The jurors leave the courtroom, throwing their final blank, disinterested glances toward the young boy. Soon after the twelve jurors are seen entering the jury room where they will begin their heated discussions and, at some point, unanimously decide the fate of the defendant.

Although the originator of the saying is unknown, the saying, "A position is what you want and an interest is why you want it,"[64] helps to define the motivation behind the jurors and why there is so much conflict between them. Looking first at Juror Eight—his position is to discuss a verdict. Moreover, Juror Eight is not committing himself to either outcome—he simply wishes to engage the jurors in conversation.

A mediator is described as a neutral third party who guides the parties through a process where they have no interest in the outcome. This process has been described in The Art and Practice of Mediation: Practice[65] as "artistry in mediation"[66] and it is described as such:

How a mediator responds to a surprising statement, an unanticipated action, a moment of uncertainty, or a particular roadblock is determined through a process of awareness—then reflection and hypothesizing —before she undertakes any action or makes any statement. To an experienced mediator, this process is often so rapid that it is reflexive .... When the process of awareness, reflection, hypothesizing, and responding takes place without pause in the mediator's actions, this is what is known as "artistry" in mediation.[67]

Henry Fonda as Juror Eight exemplifies the awareness/reflection/hypothe-

---

63   *12, supra* note 11. At 00h:01m:35s.

64   Unknown

65   Bishop, P. et all, *The Art and Practice of Mediation* 2nd ed (Toronto: Emond Montgomery Publications Limited, 2015)

66   *Ibid* at 231.

67   *Ibid.*

sizing theory mentioned above, and by doing so, he personifies an "intentional and strategic"[68] mediator.

Practice[69] suggests that a good mediator is confident, has strong leadership skills, and has the ability to guide the process of a mediation. In order for Juror Eight to achieve the first step, the awareness step, he must show that he has the capability to apply his analytical skills.

Throughout the film, Juror Eight listens carefully to the trial and the deliberations in the jury room. He is able to analyze the content by applying logic and reason. In doing so, he is able to reflect on the strengths and weaknesses of the testimony and the opinions of the jurors.

Moreover, having the natural instinct of a mediator, Juror Eight is able to draw on his knowledge of human interaction and behaviour.

There are no two scenes that better demonstrate his ability to hypothesize than two scenes found a few pages ahead. In these two examples, he baits a juror and then admits to breaking the law. While these two elements are in fact a negative attribute, it does demonstrate an understanding of the human psyche. Also mentioned in Practice is the fluidity in which the three elements—awareness, reflection, and hypothesizing—take place. This is demonstrated as Juror Eight moves with ease from one to another and there is rarely a pause or comment that suggests he is not actively listening.

Unbeknownst to Sidney Lumet's direction of 12 Angry Men,[70] he has addressed the artistry of a mediator without ever knowing it. As a result of his direction, one might ask the following questions: "Would Juror Eight make a good mediator today? And does he possess and demonstrate the necessary skills to be a neutral third party to a dispute?" It is possible that the character does demonstrate the makings of a very fine mediator, despite some very human frailties. The first element that comes to mind when assessing the role of a mediator is their use of active listening skills. Active listening skills include listening, body language, and the art of questioning. Further exploration of the mediator skills reveals the ability to remain neutral, which Juror Eight is somewhat successful at. This imperfect mediator is made not only for cinematic entertainment—it provides students the opportunity to critique and learn.

---

68   *Ibid.*

69   *Practice, supra* note 65.

70   *12, supra* note 11.

There is a lot of commotion at the beginning of the film as the jurors settle into the jury room; there is smoking, a discussion around a pending baseball game, the sound effects of a summer cold, and comments regarding the oppressive heat and lack of air conditioning. While the jurors move to their chairs, Juror Eight remains at the window, looking at the view and making no comment. At this point, we are introduced to a juror who is calm in the face of disorder. He is the last to take his seat. After the initial vote of eleven to one (he is the only person to vote not guilty), he is asked, "So? What do we do now?", to which Juror Eight replies, "I guess we talk."[71] While typically the mediator that would not engage in much discussion, Juror Eight encourages it, as demonstrated in the following dialogue:

Juror 7:	So, how come you vote not guilty?
Juror 8:	There were eleven votes for guilty. It's not easy to raise my hand and send a boy off to die without talking about it first."[72]

Further entrenching Juror Eight into the mediator role, it becomes apparent that he listened attentively to the six days of testimony in court, and relayed the details of the defendant's past in detail to his fellow jurors. Although unfamiliar with the term "position," Juror Eight clearly identifies the accused's position as miserable. His use of body language is also telling of a good mediator. For example, his tone of voice is typically calm and steady, he makes eye contact easily, and is relaxed and still. He is engaged when he is seated, as he leans forward with his hands folded over each other. While in court, he became curious as to the ability of the defence counsel to properly represent the defendant, and says to the jurors, "Those two witnesses were the entire case for the prosecution. Supposing they're wrong …could they be wrong? They're only people. People make mistakes. Could they be wrong?"[73] By asking this question, he is not only reflecting on the counsel's credibility but challenging the other jurors to do the same. This type of question is often used by a mediator when searching for further explanation—or perhaps an alternate answer.

While Juror Eight demonstrates key mediator skillsets and appears to have the ability to remain neutral, there are several times in the film that he does not.

71 *12, supra* note 11. At 00h:11m:53s.

72 *12, supra* note 11. At 00h:12m:43s.

73 *12, supra* note 11. At 00h:25m:23s.

In one instance, he wants to prove a point to Juror Three by impressing upon him the saying that, "I'll kill him" is just a figure of speech. In order to do this, he provokes Juror Three to lunge after him. The following dialogue pushes Juror Three to the point where he yells, "I'll kill him!"[74]

Juror 8:	Perhaps you'd like to pull the switch.
Juror 3:	For this kid, you bet I would!
Juror 8:	I feel sorry for you. What it must feel like to wanna pull the switch? Ever since you've walked into this room you've been acting like a self-appointed public avenger. You want to see this boy die because you personally want it, not because of the facts. You're a sadist.[75]
Juror 3:	Let me go! I'll kill him! I'll kill him!
Juror 8:	You don't really mean you'll kill me, do you?[76]

This scene, no doubt, has led to much discussion, as it demonstrates a baiting tactic which, while inappropriate for a mediator, can be used to discuss provocation and de-escalating adversarial dialogue.

Furthermore, in perhaps the most obvious violation of a mediator's neutrality, Juror Eight admits to the jurors that he went walking one evening and purchased a switchblade knife exactly like the one the defendant supposedly used to kill his father. When questioned, Juror Eight states, "That's right. I broke the law."[77] He suggests that someone else could have stabbed his father with a similar knife. Although his intent was to suggest a possibility that someone else might have committed the murder, he broke the law in doing so, and so challenged his neutrality.

Even with those two challenges in mind, it would be more than plausible to believe that Juror Eight, in today's day and age, would make an excellent mediator, despite his frailties.[78]

12 Angry Men[79] appeals to Kolb's accommodator style as a learner and an

. . . .

74   *12, supra* note 11. At 00h:59m:03s.

75   *12, supra* note 11. At 00h:59m:05s.

76   *12, supra* note 11. At 00h:59m:07s.

77   *Ibid.*

78   *Lightstone, supra* note 62.

79   *12, supra* note 11.

apprentice perspective as an instructor, as it promotes discussion around a skillset and allows the student to model that example.

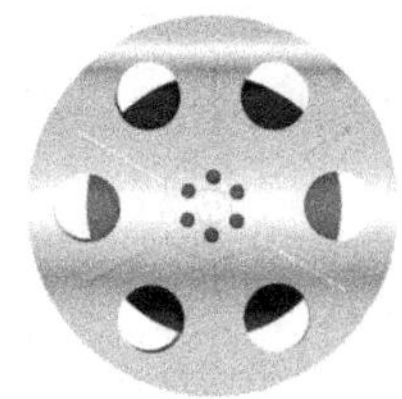

ARBITRATION

The 2015 film Woman in Gold[80] is the last in the trio of films that address conflict resolution methods as noted on the Appropriate Dispute Resolution Continuum[81] and introduced in Introduction to Dispute Resolution.[82] This film demonstrates a power-based process (the commandeering of property by the Nazis in WWII) in which a panel of three arbitrators are chosen to award an outcome of a major art restitution lawsuit. The arbitration removes the power from the parties to resolve the dispute and leaves it entirely in the hands of the arbitral panel. It is important to note that this film is a biography based on the real-life story of Maria

---

80   *Woman, supra* note 13.

81   *Introduction, supra* note 19.

82   *Ibid.*

Altmann. Its purpose within the context of this paper is to introduce the student to arbitration as an option in dispute resolution without citing examples directly from the film, as in the two examples above, with the Tenth Man[83] and 12 Angry Men,[84] and within the following films discussed in the paper, with the exception of Colonia.[85] While Woman in Gold[86] demonstrates a historical journey that leads Maria Altmann from the possibility of court to an arbitration panel, this paper draws comparisons from the textbook Dispute Resolution Reading[87] and other sources to highlight the use of arbitration as a dispute resolution option— in this example, within the art restitution community.

Students who are assimilators would enjoy Woman in Gold[88] due to their aptitude for extrapolating concepts (in this example, arbitration) and applying it to present-day life scenarios. Pratt suggests that instructors who are concerned with social reform would use a film such as Woman in Gold[89] to best demonstrate "how the selected group was impacted [and how] power differences are explored."[90]

• • •

In 1903, Ferdinand Bloch-Bauer, a wealthy Austrian industrialist and sugar manufacturer, commissioned Gustav Klimt (1862–1918) to paint his beautiful wife, Adele Bloch-Bauer. The first painting of Adele Bloch-Bauer was called Adele Bloch-Bauer I,[91] and the second portrait was called, Adele Bloch-Bauer II,[92] and was painted by Klimt in 1912. Between the years of 1903 and 1918, the Bloch-

---

83   *Tenth, supra* note 12.

84   *12, supra* note 11.

85   *Colonia, supra* note 16.

86   *Woman, supra* note 13.

87   *Dispute Resolution Readings, supra* note 40.

88   *Woman, supra* note 13.

89   *Ibid.*

90   *Lights, supra* note 30.

91   Gustav Klimt, "Adele Bloch-Bauer 1" (1907), online: <https://www.google.com/search?sourceid=navclient&aq=&oq=Gustav+Klimt+Paintings&ie=UTF8&rlz=1T4TSCA_enCA456CA456&q=Gustav+Klimt+Paintings&gs_l=hp...0i131j0l4.0.0.0.4858.   0.lx50ctcT-Q4>

92   Gustav Klimt, "Adele Bloch-Bauer 11" (1912), online: <https://www.google.com/search?sourceid=navclient&aq=&oq=Gustav+Klimt+Paintings&ie=UTF8&rlz=1T4TSCA_e nCA456CA456&q=Gustav+Klimt+Paintings&gs_l=hp...0i131j0l4.0.0.0.4858   0.lx50ctcT-Q4>

Bauers, purchased six Gustav Klimt paintings, including the most famous portrait, Adele Bloch-Bauer I,[93] also called Woman in Gold.[94] The Klimt paintings were only a few of the works of art and other relevant pieces expropriated by the Nazis during WWII.

The timeline depicting major events leading up to the three-panel arbitration creates a narrative ripe to produce thought-provoking dialogue. In 1923, Adele Bloch-Bauer created a will that asked her husband to leave the Klimt paintings to the Austrian National Gallery only after his death. Subsequently, in 1925, Adele died of meningitis. Thereafter, Klimt paintings and other valuable art pieces were confiscated in 1938 by the Nazis. They were then displayed at the Austrian National Gallery or distributed amongst prominent Nazi leaders. Following the war's end, Ferdinand died in 1945, leaving his estate to his nephew and his two nieces, one of whom was Maria Altmann. However, the Klimt paintings were never included in Ferdinand Bloch-Bauer's estate, as Ferdinand Bloch-Bauer believed they no longer belonged to him.

The Austrian Annulment Act of May 1946[95] declared all transactions (confiscation of art and property) under the jurisdiction of the Nazis null and void. This included the exchange of valuable pieces of art "in favour of the Austrian public museum and in the name of preserving national heritage"[96] in exchange for exit visas. Even though the paintings were already in the hands of the Austrian National Gallery, the Bloch-Bauer family lawyer agreed to surrender the paintings in exchange.

In 1998, under allegations of Nazi pillaging, "the Austrian Government opened its archives to permit research on the provenance of the national collection …and soon passed the Restitution Act.[97] In addition, a Restitution Committee was created to review each of the restitution requests."[98] When the

93   *Klimt, supra* note 91.

94   Woman in Gold appears to be an unofficial title of Adele Bloch-Bauer 1

95   *"Annulment Act",* (15 May 1946), online: <http://www.ris.bka.gv.at/Dokumente/BgblPdf/1946_106_0/1946_106_0.pdf>

96   *Caroline Renold,* 2012

97   *"Restitution Act"* (4 December 1998), online: http://www.ris.bka.gv.at/Dokumente/BgblPdf/1998_181_1/1998_181_1.pdf

98   Caroline Renold, Alessandro Chechi, Anne Laure Bandle, Marc-André Renold, "Case Six Klimt Paintings – Maria Altmann and Austria," online: (2012) Arthemis Art-Law Centre University of Geneva https://plone.unige.ch/art-adr/cases-affaires/6-klimt-paintings-2013-maria-altmann-and-austria/case-note-

window opened, Austrian journalist Hubertus Czernin[99] discovered that Ferdinand Bloch-Bauer did not donate the Klimt paintings, but that they had been removed by the Nazis, supported by the Austrian regime. The Restitution Ac1[100] would also address those parties who donated artwork in exchange for export permits and wished to seek restitution.

In the film Woman in Gold,[101] Maria Altmann asks her new, inexperienced lawyer, Randol Schoenberg...[102]

Maria Altmann:	What do you know about art restitution?
Randol Schoenberg:	Not a thing.
Maria Altmann:	Then it's never too late to learn.[103]

Under the Restitution Act, Maria Altmann "requested the restitution of the Klimt paintings ...but [it] was rejected in 1999."[104] At this point, Maria Altmann decided to challenge the decision in Austria, but due to the Austrian court demanding the legal fees up front (a percentage of the value of the claim), she withdrew. In 2000, after returning to the States, she "sue[d] the Republic of Austria and the Austrian National Gallery, alleging expropriation of property in violation of international law."[105] The motion by the defendants (the Republic of Austria), was denied based on the Foreign Sovereign Immunities Act (FSIA) of 1976.[106]

"The FSIA governs all litigation in both state and federal courts against foreign states and governments, including their "agencies and instrumentalities."[107] Under

----

2013-six-klimt-paintings-2013-maria-altmann-and-austria

99   It became Hubertus Cernan's personal mission to reunite artwork confiscated by the Nazi's to its original owners. He did this to compensate and make amends to those who were impacted by the activities of his Nazi father.

100 *Restitution, supra* note 118.

101 *Woman, supra* note 13.

102 Randol Schoenberg went on to open a law firm focusing on art restitution.

103 *Woman, supra* note 13. At 00h:05m:37s.

104 *Restitution, supra* note 97.

105 *Ibid.*

106 Stewart, D. P. "The Foreign Sovereign Immunities Act: A Guide for Judges. Georgetown University Law Center, Federal Judicial Center International Litigation Guide".

107 *Ibid.*

"C. Basic Rules of Application 2, Retroactivity,"[108] Maria Altmann was allowed to sue, even though the occurrence took place before FSIA was created. In 2004, Maria Altmann was permitted to start a civil action in US Federal Court for the return of five of the six Klimt paintings. With the defeat in US Federal Court, the Austrian Republic agreed to binding arbitration in Austria, and, in 2006, the arbitral panel ruled in favour of Maria Altmann, returning five Gustav Klimt paintings to her.[109]

When deciding to arbitrate, an agreement must be reached on what the arbitration will look like. For example, it was decided that each party would have an arbitrator of their choice and a third arbitrator, who would be neutral. The parties agreed

> [The] arbitration court should reach its decision pursuant to the provisions of Austrian substantive and procedural law … in legal terms, its decision was based solely on the facts presented to it by the parties on the basis of the evidence they submitted …the arbitration court's decision had to be based exclusively on legal criteria. They were assigned total jurisdiction, with the proceeding to be conducted according to the arbitration court's discretion; this was not objected to by the parties.[110]

This is demonstrated in the film when Randol Schoenberg's character, Randy, suggests,

> "Arbitration in Vienna—we choose one of the arbitrators, you choose the other, the third is neutral."[111]

According to Dispute Resolution Readings,[112] the wording of the agreement is

108 *Ibid.*

109 There was sound reason to believe that the sixth of the Gustav Klimt painting was sold to friends of Ferdinand and Adele Bloch-Bauer and was not confiscated.

110 *Maria V. Altmann, Francis Gutmann, Trevor Mantle, and George Bentley, Dr. Nelly Auersperg, v. the Republic of Austria* (2006) (Arbitration, Vienna Austria) (Arbitrators: Dr. Andreas Nödl, Lawyer Professor Walter H. Rechberger, Professor Peter Rummel (Chairman).

111 *Woman, supra* note 13. At 01h:21m:49s.

112 *Dispute Resolution, supra* note 40 at 529.

crucial to a successful arbitration and, as Dispute Resolution Readings[113] suggests, the arbitration agreement addressed the number of arbitrators, the rules of its implementation, the power, and the ability to apply an award. This is important for the dispute resolution students to understand, as it demonstrates a less formal, rights-based process whereby both parties have the ability to create the terms of the arbitration.

While the audience is briefly introduced to the arbitration panel, its main objective is to ascertain who owned all six of the Klimt paintings and whether or not Adele Bloch-Bauer's will was binding. "The panel concluded that the will was not legally binding for Ferdinand Bloch-Bauer. More specifically, the arbitral panel held that the clause regarding the Klimt paintings was merely a request which Ferdinand Bloch-Bauer had publicly agreed to fulfill."[114] Therefore, as Adele Bloch-Bauer never actually owned the paintings, and her husband always had, the Austrian Gallery had no legal right to them. In the paper, Case Six Klimt Paintings – Maria Altmann and Austria, Caroline Renold et al.,[115] the restitution of the paintings is described as such:

> The arbitral held that the paintings Adele Bloch-Bauer I, Adele Bloch-Bauer II, Buchenwald, Häuser in Unterach am Attersee, and Apfelbaum I were to be handed over to Maria Altmann, and that the painting Amalie Zuckerkandl was the Property of the Republic of Austria. Austria paid the cost of the arbitration.[116]

However, those who had their property confiscated but did not have the means or the wherewithal to seek restitution, found themselves lost in a maze.

> Know[ing] the exact address and the date the apartment was looted, but [the] descriptions of the items are almost generic, and one cannot necessarily find an eighteenth-century style lady's writing table, inlaid and with ormolu mounts. It matches too many desks ….[117]

113 *Ibid.*

114 *Reynold, supra note 98.*

115 *Ibid.*

116 *Ibid.*

117 Constance Lowenthal, "Recovering Looted Jewish Cultural Property", online: (2004) 7:6 Permanent Court of Arbitration < https://pca-cpa.org/en/home/ >.

In addition, paintings are more easily identified, but artists frequently painted the same subjects over and over …in the absence of measurements and photographs, most people's description …simply fall short.[118]

In another example,

> An elderly woman who saw paintings in her uncle's Paris apartment …believe[s] she should be able to find and recover the paintings based …having heard of the Nazis' efficiency …she believes that the officials …are hiding essential information from her when they say they cannot help. [No] one explained to her that her lack of detailed information …was an insurmountable problem.[119]

In a response to the growing need for restitution, the Journal of International Commercial Law and Technology[120] published an article called "Alternative Dispute Resolution and Art Law: A New Research Project of the Geneva Art-Law Centre"[121] (Research Project).[122] The purpose of the Research Project launched in 2010 is to

> …create an Art-Law ADR Database that would provide a record of art-law disputes worldwide, which were resolved by means of ADR methods …and the project aims to examine which types of ADR mechanism are used in art-law disputes, and which are decisive criteria that have led parties to opt for out-of-court settlement.[123]

The research project[124] was prepared in three stages: a database was collected for

---

118 *Ibid.*

119 *Ibid.*

120 Anne Laure Bandle, Sarah Theurich, "Alternative Dispute Resolution and Art-Law - a New Research Project of the Geneva Art-Law Centre", online: (2011) Retrieved from Journal of International Commercial Law and Technology: https://www.neliti.com/publications/28706/alternative-dispute-resolution-and-art-law-a-new-research-project-of-the-geneva

121 *Ibid.*

122 It is important to note, that the *Research Report* is the opinion of its author only.

123 *Research Project, supra* note 120.

124 *Ibid.*

information on "art-law cases resolved through ADR," [125] the next stage analyzed the information, and the last stage addressed the research in upcoming "conferences and made available in [appropriate publications.]" [126]

As art is connected to "creation, exhibition, reproduction, sale, and transfer of property of both works of art and cultural objects" and concerns "legal fields as varied as international law, property law, copyright, insurance, customs and tax law," [127] it also involves parties from different backgrounds with different values. The author suggests that "art-law" [128] disputes are more suitable to ADR than a rights-based process. Arbitration, for example, may allow a dispute to resolve issues of different jurisdictions quicker and in a mutual location. Furthermore, parties to an "art-law" [129] conflict may choose an arbitrator who [has] "expertise of the art-law [130] issues at stake and an understanding of the cultural backgrounds. Therefore, parties could appoint a mediator or arbitrator who is a specialist in art-restitution nuances." [131] The research project [132] also outlines other benefits, such as unique resolutions that could incorporate "specific ownership agreements, the conclusion of loan agreements, donations, the withdrawal of a restitution claim in exchange for a monetary compensation, etc." [133] A decade or so earlier, S. Ware wrote in their article "Arbitration and Assimilation," [134]

> Arbitration can produce a sophisticated, comprehensive legal system. Even better, it can produce many such systems. [135] The article suggests that should the arbitrators be in the field of the

125 *Ibid.*

126 *Ibid.*

127 *Ibid.*

128 *Ibid.*

129 *Ibid.*

130 *Ibid.*

131 *Ibid.*

132 *Ibid.*

133 *Ibid.*

134 Stephen J. Ware, "Arbitration and Assimilation", 7:4 Washington University Law Review online: (1999) <https://journals.library.wustl.edu/lawreview/article/id/5933/

135 *Ibid.*

area they are arbitrating, they would be more inclined to understand the nuances of the dispute.

S. Ware sees this as a great advantage. Should the arbitration be amongst a common group, then it could create its own privatized law.[136] The growth of ADR for art law creates a new dimension to the pedagogy, and this film creates a lens through which students can be exposed to this recent development.

Aligning with the 1998 Washington Conference on Holocaust-Era Assets,[137] the conference recognize[d] that, among participating nations, there are differing legal systems and that countries act within the context of their own laws. As such, eleven principles were endorsed for "dealing with Nazi-looted art."[138] Section 3.2 of the research report[139] acknowledges Principle 11: "Nations are encouraged to develop national processes to implement these principles, particularly as they relate to alternative dispute resolution mechanisms for resolving ownership issues."[140]

However, as there were many who were unable to move forward with restitution, the research report[141] refers to Maria Altmann's arbitration case as pivotal, as it opened the door

> [to] other Holocaust victims, [to] seek redress in US courts for the restitution of artworks .... In deciding to withdraw the state's immunity, the US Supreme Court reversed years of precedent to the contrary ... and open[ed] the door to other suits against foreign nations in US courts.[142]

Klimt painted using gold leaf and modelled his work after Japanese pillar prints, making him one of the most successful Art Nouveau artists in Austria. "He is

---

136 *Ibid*

137 Stuart E. Eizenstat, "In Support of Principles on Nazi-Confiscated Art: Holocaust-Era Assets" (Presentation) delivered at the Washington Conference, 3 December 1998)

138 Washington Conference Principles on Nazi-Confiscated Art", online: Commission for Looted Art in Europe: <http://www.lootedartcommission.com/home>.

139 *Research Report, supra* note 120.

140 *Washington, supra* note 134.

141 *Research Report, supra* note 120.

142 *Woman, supra* note 13.

remembered as one of the greatest decorative painters of the twentieth century, and he also produced one of the century's most significant bodies of erotic art."[143] Klimt paintings were sold to Ronald S. Lauder in 2006 for $135 million.

Woman in Gold[144] demonstrates a power-based process in which a panel of three arbitrators are chosen to award an outcome of a major art restitution lawsuit. Its purpose within the context of this paper is to introduce the assimilator style student to arbitration as an option in dispute resolution. Pratt suggests that instructors who are concerned with social reform (such as the ability to seek redress from other nations) would use a film such as Woman in Gold[145] to best demonstrate "critical examples of power and …how the selected group was impacted [and how] power differences are explored."[146]

143 Unknown, "Gustav Klimt, Austrian Painter" (Unknown), The Art Story, Modern Art Insight, online: <www.theartstory.org/artist-klimt-gustav.htm>

144 *Woman, supra* note 13.

145 *Ibid.*

146 *Lights, supra* note 30.

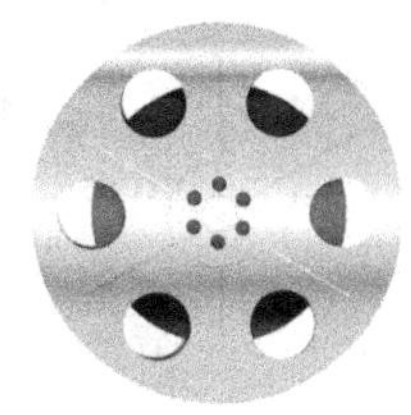

THEORY AND PRACTICE OF DISPUTE RESOLUTION[147]

Music from the Big House[148] is a musical documentary featuring Rita Chiarelli[149] performing in Louisiana with jazz and blues musicians in a unique environment with a unique group of men. The initial incentive for her multiple trips to Louisiana was to research the roots of blues music. Instead, what she found during her numerous trips to the state was a rich musical history not only in Louisiana, but inside one of Louisiana's worst prisons, Angola.

147 *Theory, supra* note 6.

148 *Music, supra* note 15.

149 Canada's lead female blues singer, Juno award winner

Lights[150] suggests that a nurturing teaching perspective addresses students of varying degrees of knowledge and builds in difficulty throughout the content. In the example of Music,[151] students may facilitate small group conversations around the multi-layered components of the film. These concepts could include music and its healing nature, religion, and the concept of restorative justice. The focus of the nurturing perceptive is to allow students to learn from each other. The divergent learning style, according to Kolb, "prefers to gather information and use imagination to solve problems. They are best at viewing concrete situations [from] several different viewpoints …prefer to work in groups, [and] to listen with an open mind."[152] These students would best benefit from a scaffolding learning experience that builds on pre-existing content, such as the concepts mentioned above.

Howard Zehr, in his book Changing Lenses: A New Focus for Crime and Justice,[153] addresses the multi-definitions of the word shalom, and how it impacts the concept of restoration. His approach is from both an Old Testament and New Testament perspective. The first definition of shalom intends that people should live with "health and material property."[154] The second meaning of shalom implies that everyone should live in peace (even with conflict). The final meaning of shalom recommends that we move forward with "honesty and moral integrity."[155] As each of the definitions is meant to address God's intent, we may be able to extrapolate that God's further meaning of the word shalom also includes change, forgiveness, redemption, and justice. Zehr suggests that there is no shalom when the three pieces of its definition are not together.

In the New Testament, teaching focuses on the relationship "of peace between people and God, and between people themselves on a variety of levels."[156] As

150 *Lights, supra* note 30.

151 *Music, supra* note 15.

152 Unknown, "David Kolb's Learning Styles Model and Experiential Learning Theory (ELT)" (March 2017) online: https://www.businessballs.com/self-awareness/kolbs-learning styles/#:~:text=Diverging%20(feeling%20and%20watching%20%2D%20CE,situations%20from%20several%20different%20viewpoints.

153 Howard Zehr, *Changing Lenses: A New Focus for Crime and Justice* (Waterloo, ON: Herald Press, 2005).

154 *Ibid* at 131.

155 *Ibid.*

156 *Ibid* at 132.

Christ reflected these beliefs in his teachings, Zehr suggests,

> Jesus came so that things might be as they ought to be both
> among people and between people and God, and even nature.
> Thus, reconciliation is an important theme in the New Testa-
> ment, but the state of all rightness which God intends continues
> to have the material and physical dimensions that it had in the
> Old Testament.[157]

Furthermore, Zehr indicates that all parties to a crime have the opportunity to "go home satisfied,"[158] and uses Exodus 18:23 of the Old Testament to support his statement. It says, "If thou shalt do this thing, and God command thee so, then thou shalt be able to endure, and all this people shall also go to their place in peace."[159]

As the audience views Music,[160] we are drawn into the stories and the joyful and haunting melodies shared with us. We find ourselves on a journey with the inmates as their stories unfold, and we listen as they come to terms with what they have done and how they found themselves in what is described as "one the bloodiest places in the United States."[161] In addition, Rita Chiarelli finds herself at odds with her once-clear values—now at stake—as she comes to know her fellow performers as warm and caring souls who share her love of music, yet have taken the lives of others or committed other criminal offences. We also allow ourselves to be drawn into the redemptive stories of Wayne Guidry, Ray Jones, Emanuel Lee, Matthew Morgan, Albert Patterson, Prentice Robinson, and Laird Veillon, and we challenge our own values. Should a life sentence really mean life in all cases? Is there any opportunity for redemption? Is there any opportunity to repair harm caused in both a restorative justice approach and in a biblical approach—both as suggested by Zehr?

Giving an answer to the question of redemption, Zehr said, "Victim/offender mediation falls under the restorative justice umbrella." Restorative justice may be viewed as a process that "puts the needs of those touched by crime—rather than

---

157 *Ibid.*

158 *Ibid* at 141

159 "Exodus 18 King James Version (KJV)" online: Exodus 18: https://www.biblegateway.com/passage/?search=Exodus+18&version=KJV>.

160 *Music, supra* note 15.

161 *Music, supra* note 15. At 00h:26m:14s.

the institutional needs of the state—at the centre of the process."[162] Furthermore, Changing Lenses[163] compares a retributive model of resolution to a restorative justice model, and refers to both as "lenses." For example, through a retributive lens, the criminal system has the following perspectives: fixes blame, focuses on the past, is adversarial, imposes punishment, the victims' truth is secondary and their suffering is usually ignored, there is no responsibility for resolution, and there is little restitution. With a restorative justice lens, there is an interest in solving the problem, there is focus on the future, restoration is significant, the victims are given their chance to share their stories, and the offender not only is responsible, but is given a role in the resolution. The differences in the two processes could also be evaluated by addressing what law was broken, who broke it, how should the offender be punished (retributive), who has been hurt, what the victim's needs are, and who is responsible for making it right (restorative)."[164] In Music[165] none of the Angola inmates is ever provided the opportunity to have a victim-offender dialogue; as Albert Patterson points out, the state of Louisiana does not provide for that opportunity.

In Barb Toews's book The Little Book of Restorative Justice for People in Prison,[166] Toews suggests that when a crime has been committed, restorative justice includes the victims, offenders, the families of both, as well as the community—and that the following needs of all must be met. Restorative justice would address "who has been hurt, what does he/she need, who should be involved in meeting those needs, and what is the best way to repair the harm ...."[167] Zehr, in Changing Lenses[168] adds to Toews recommendations: "obligations resulting from those harms, and the [use] of inclusive, collaborative processes."[169] Zehr places particular emphasis on the following principles: obligations, inclusive, and collaborative—suggesting that the offender must take responsibility (a cornerstone of the restorative justice concept) and accountability.

162 *Changing Lenses, supra* note 174.

163 *Changing Lenses, supra* note 174.

164 Helen Lightstone, "When Security is Ready" (2016) 13.

165 *Music, supra* note 15.

166 Toews, B. The Little Book of Restorative Justice for People in Prison. (Intercourse, PA, USA: Good BPPKS, (2006).

167 *Ibid* at 21.

168 *Changing Lenses, supra* note 174.

169 *Changing Lenses, supra* note 174 at 270.

Inclusivity addresses the need for victims to participate, and "collaborative" suggests the need for everyone to work together to restore and heal all parties as best as possible.

Little Book[170] looks closely at how the community, victims, families, and the offenders move forward after a crime has been committed. It suggests that there are two types of communities: the people close to the offender and the general community itself. Members of a community may have specific needs in repairing harm caused—for example, a group might have a need to ensure community safety, while someone directly impacted may have needs that focus on themselves. The book further suggests that when a crime has been committed, it is because something is wrong with the community, and therefore creates an obligation on the community towards the person who caused harm. The intent is to "[move] from destructive to positive values …when a community sees the worth in each member and works for the good of all members."[171] To assist in strengthening each person impacted by crime, eight elements help them make sense of what took place. They include "relationship and safety, empowerment, storytelling and venting feelings, information, growth and accountability."[172] These are referred to as "individual justice needs."[173]

Looking at the victim's needs, Little Book[174] suggests that restoring safety and relationship is first; this includes physical safety and emotional safety. While physical safety might include changing a lock, emotional safety might include the need to be believed. As the book suggests, this leads to empowerment. Information is also important, as it might include answers to questions, such as "why did this happen to me?"[175] Storytelling is also central, and is the only reference to victims in Music.[176] Albert Patterson says of the victims' family who spoke at his parole hearing in 2004:

Whatever they had in their mind and heart from the beginning,

170 *Little Book, supra* note 187 at 25.

171 *Little Book, supra* note 187 at 29.

172 *Ibid.*

173 *Little Book, supra* note 187 at 33.

174 *Little Book, supra* note 187 at 39.

175 Mediation - A Somali family where the mother was concerned that her family was being targeted.

176 *Music, supra* note 15.

> I destroyed it, and I only have me to blame, …but at least I know
> one thing, their words came out of their mouths, that [they]
> came here to forgive [me], but after hearing what [I] had to say
> …and we have to leave here and go to the graveyard and visit
> our family, and he got all his family here.[177]

In addition to the storytelling component of the parole hearing, his victim's families address accountability and validation. In having the opportunity to be present at a parole hearing, the victim's family also obtains information that could help explain questions such as what happened and why.

> Albert Patterson: The only thing we can say is: "No, we don't want him out now. We don't want him to die there."[178]

During Music,[179] there are only two instances where we see the family and friends of the offenders at Angola. The first instance is at a meal in the cafeteria, before Rita Chiarelli and the three bands perform for the rest of the men and their guests. The men, in a separate area, are patted down and then released into the dining hall to meet their families, who are carrying food, paintings, letters, and small wishing-wells, and are in search of their loved ones. Hugs are being exchanged, stories are being told, people are praying over their meals and people are eating.

Someone calls to Ray, "Ray!"[180] To which Ray replies, "Hey Guy, what's happening?"[181] Ray searches for his wife, who is at the back of the cafeteria, waiting for him with open arms—it is a warm and loving embrace.

• • •

The second instance is the performance itself, where everyone enjoys the music of Rita Chiarelli and the three groups performing. From the activity in the dining hall and sanctuary where the performance will take place, it is clear that the sense of normalcy is important to all, even though everyone is under the watchful eye of the guards observing. That being said, it is apparent that both venues have provided a location for the inmates to feel cared for by their families, and, in

---

177 *Music, supra* note 15. At 01h:09m:35s.

178 *Music, supra* note 15. At 01h:09m:37s.

179 *Music, supra* note 15.

180 *Music, supra* note 34. At 00h:39m:31s.

181 *Music, supra* note 34. At 00h:39m:34s.

return, provide a sense of security to the families from knowing their loved ones are alright. This unseen exchange allows for everyone to "maintain trusting, honest, and empathetic relationships with the offender," [182] particularly when the families face a lack of control when their loved ones are incarcerated."[183]

Many of the songs performed at Angola Prison were written by Rita Chiarelli or other mainstream blues and jazz performers. The music provided a catharsis for not only the families and friends but the men as well. With melancholy song titles such as "I Love You Still"[184] and the soul-lifting "Glory, Glory,"[185] family members are able to release their emotions through music and storytelling. Further to this, the family and friends can feel growth as they attempt to heal their relationship by strengthening their broken bonds.

While the family members are gathering in the cafeteria, a young family is posing for a photographer. The canvas backdrop for the shoot is a tranquil garden, and the family is sitting on a garden bench similar to what you would find in any park or back garden. Contrast to the pleasant photographic setting is what is behind the backdrop: concrete walls, prison guards, and iron bars. However, despite the apparent disconnect, this family is struggling to maintain its unity and find meaning and accountability to move forward.

Even though the audience meets the inmates of Angola in a documentary during their incarceration, Music[186] addresses the justice needs of the offenders in the same eight elements mentioned earlier. The first reference to the justice needs of the offender is relationship and safety. Moreover, those two concepts may be extrapolated from this quote: "Programs can't rehabilitate; you have to rehabilitate yourself."[187] In order to rehabilitate, the inmates need to be supported by others, so that they are in a better position to become accountable for their crimes. Ray Jones addressed his own rehabilitation because of the relationship he had with another inmate years before:[188]

. . . .

182 *Little Book, supra* note 187 at 52.

183 This is mainly due to the regulations of the prison system.

184 Rita Chiarelli, "*Music from the Big House "Soundtrack*," CD: I Love You Still. (Louisiana State Prison, Toronto, Mad Iris Music Inc. 2011).

185 Rita Chiarelli, "*Music from the Big House "Soundtrack*," CD: Glory, Glory. (Louisiana State Prison, Toronto, Mad Iris Music Inc. 2011).

186 *Music, supra* note 15.

187 *Ibid.*

188 It is not clear if the inmate has been released or is currently incarcerated.

It's based upon who you get in contact with. And see, if you get
in contact with the bad crowd, then you just eventually follow
a bad route. I was fortunate to find a guy that was uh …did
some time here …. You've got a life sentence, you want to do
some good time, stay away from all the foolishness …stay away
from all that. And uh, he gave me some good pointers on that,
and I took his advice, and uh …I needed to know the way
another way, and I had an opportunity …he cared enough to
share that with me, and I was listening. And likewise, I give
that back …. In the law library, they always talkin' to me because
they got some type of problem they have, so a conversation
going to kick off.[189]

Ray Jones, who had already taken responsibility for his actions, confirms his
accountability in the following statement:

You know, I'm a firm believer drugs and alcohol is the energy
behind crime. If you think that's not real, you just ask anyone
in there what they did, and I'll guarantee you [unintelligible],
rob, steal, ste—and kill and destroy. You start with me, I killed
somebody. Ignorantly. For the drugs. On that state, you could
do anything; you harm people that you love.[190]

In addition, Matthew Morgan says this about accountability after fifteen years
of incarceration:

But as you grow older, you [begin][191] to put that aside, and you
[begin] to look at your life, and you [begin] to realize that
morality is, is really, it's not just a saying, it's not just a word, it's
important. It's not moral to rape. It's not moral to murder, or to
steal, or to be a manipulator, or to do things that are not, um,
right, in society. But you can't just let somebody tell you that,
you've got to experience it for yourself and if you [begin] to
make moral decisions, you [begin] to see a change in your life,

---

189 *Music, supra* note 15. At 00h:24m:23s.

190 *Music, supra* note 15. At 01h:05m:06s.

191 The accent was very difficult to decipher between 'begin and began.' The paper
moves forward with the choice to say 'began.'

you [begin] to be able to hold on to your money, you [begin] to be able to restore relationships with your children and your parents and with the people here, they [begin] to see that change. It's not just talk, you see what I'm saying, 'cause you're living that walk? And then, the warden [comes] and his philosophy opens up that door for you to walk through and to [begin to rebuild your life].[192]

Storytelling and feelings are predominant in the film, as it provides the opportunity for the men to express themselves in song, sharing their fears and their concerns "before, during, and after the crime."[193] Rita Chiarelli discusses the impact of music on her, and in her haunting song, "These Four Walls,"[194] Rita Chiarelli evokes the loneliness of those spending time in prison. Her words reach down to the very soul of the person, drawing out pain, frustration, and despair:

> You see these bars, you see these chains,
> You think you don't know me, I have no name,
> Cause all I have are these four walls,
> Yah, these four walls, these four walls
>
> ...
>
> I had a wife, I had a son
> And they were hungry, and I had a gun
> And I saw that man, yes, I did, I watched him die
> I took his life, his life took mine
>
> Forgiveness, Lord, forgiveness, Lord,
> On this earth, on this earth, don't come
> Ahh, not 'til they lay you down, one 'side one
> So, take me now, Lord, take me now, Lord
> 'Cause all I have are these four walls, these four walls[195]

192 *Music, supra* note 15. At 00h:48m:22s.

193 *Little Book, supra* note 187 at 47.

194 Rita Chiarelli, *"Music from the Big House "Soundtrack,"* CD: These Four Wall. (Louisiana State Prison, Toronto, Mad Iris Music Inc. 2011).

195 *Ibid.*

While interviewed during Music,[196] Rita Chiarelli said,

> …and then you realize it gives you power on the inside, power
> to set you free, power to release your anger, and you know the
> uplifting, the spiritual uplifting, and the emotional uplifting,
> you know, um, that music gave me And, um, it changed, it
> changed who I was—I could release all of that in my singing.[197]

However, storytelling and feelings can easily be applied to the men at Angola. Wayne Guidry says this about writing the blues: "And so I think in the music that I write when I'm going through the blues, that's what I'm looking for—I'm looking for the answer, I'm looking for the hope, and I hear it in the music." [198]

Furthering a need for information, Ray Jones works in the prison law library, assisting parties who need help by providing them support and counselling. At the time of filming, he had been incarcerated for approximately thirty years, with no hope of being released. Rita Chiarelli states that when you get a life sentence in Louisiana, it is a life sentence. Ray Jones furthered his strength by creating Pure Heart Ministries220[199] in order to assist others. By doing so, he created a path for himself that will ease him through the hardships of his life sentence. Furthermore, once Ray Jones accepted the words of wisdom from his friend and chose to live his life in a different manner, he created new values for himself. Having created a new path and new values, he provided himself the opportunity to grow and move forward.

As noted in the introduction, there is much discussion around the concept of the New and the Old Testament, shalom, and restitution. It would be remiss not to mention how faith has impacted the inmates featured in the film, and its overarching impact on their restorative journey—despite the fact that most of the men will never be released. Emanuel Lee says the following with respect to faith:

> "This used to be one of the bloodiest places in the United States.
> Now, they walkin' with Bibles in their hands …but you don't
> hear a whole lot of fighting, and they having conversations

---

196 *Music, supra* note 15.

197 *Music, supra* note 15. At 00h:33m:53s.

198 *Music, supra* note 15. At 00h:52m:45s.

199 *Music, supra* note 15.

about the Word, and that's a big change."[200]

Ray Jones says also addresses his faith in the following few sentences:

> I thought everything I need—I thought I at least need to be
> high to do it …. I made a lot of choices, but I only made one
> good one, that's when I received Christ as my lord and saviour.
> You know, being in a place like this, Angola, and then going …
> you gonna need a saviour, you need someone to save you,
> because you gonna need some help—it's real. You know when
> it come real? When it get in you. It's not a Sunday thing; it
> works on Monday, too, all the way to Friday and Saturday and
> Sunday. You go to live it ….[201]

Were it not for the faith each of these men have, their journey at Angola would
be insurmountable. Faith provides them the relationship and safety by way of
support, accountability for their actions, storytelling, and venting. By way of their
music, and by the means of Christ's teachings, they have found a way to see out
the remainder of their time.

Rita Chiarelli also finds herself on a journey questioning her values, recognizing the victims and questioning whether forgiveness could ever be in her heart.
Even though these men made mistakes, she believes that there is room for forgiveness and that they are changed men, even though they did horrific crimes. Perhaps
the wisest comment that Rita Chiarelli makes is the most restorative—and the
comment that brings the most shalom:

> It's opened my heart a lot more to understanding who we are,
> all of us, and how these people, keeping these people, um, angry,
> and keeping them resentful, hurts all society, hurts all of us—
> because when we are out there, we think we are not affected,
> but we are, because that anger, that hate, um, you know, is
> brought down to their children and their children, to their
> wives and to their families—it just perpetuates, you know, and
> um, that's one thing I really didn't expect to have happen
> to me.[202]

---

200 *Music, supra* note 15. At 01h:02m:293s

201 *Music, supra* note 15. At 01h:05m:06s.

202 *Music, supra* note 15. At 01h:02m:293s.

The following quote from Arthur Lockhart and Lynn Zammits's *Restorative Justice: Transforming Society*[203] asks, "We must ask ourselves the question: If punishment wasn't an option, what would we do?"[204] This question challenges the community to re-think how to move forward when challenged. What would society do to repair the harm caused? By having the necessary parties involved in the resolution, without leaning towards a retributive, punishment-based solution, it is possible proper healing could take place. As mentioned in Burning Bridges,[205] "This question may lead us into a very different direction."[206] In the film. an unidentified community member says during a sentencing conference,[207] "It takes a village to raise a child. It sure looks like this village didn't do a very good job."[208]

Lights[209] suggests that a nurturing teaching perspective addresses students of varying degrees of knowledge as it scaffolds pre-existing content and helps students learn from each other. The divergent learning style is best "at viewing concrete situations [from] several different viewpoints …the divergent student prefers to work in groups and to listen with an open mind. Furthermore, these people perform better in situations that require ideas-generation, for example, brainstorming."[210] Music[211] provides an opportunity for students to facilitate small group conversations around the multi-layered components of the film. These concepts could include music and its healing nature, religion, and the concept of restorative justice, with particular focus on the eight elements of individual justice needs as seen through the eyes of all parties involved in a crime.

---

203 Art Lockhart & Lynn Zammit, *Restorative Justice: Transforming Society* (Toronto, ON: Inclusion Press, 2005).

204 *Ibid*, at 68.

205 *Burning Bridges*, DVD (The International Institute for Restorative Practices, 2011).

206 *Ibid.*

207 This true story addresses six young men who burn down a covered bridge in a picturesque American town. A sentencing conference was facilitated to address the harm to all involved.

208 *Burning Bridges, supra* note 199. At: 00h:15m: 36s.

209 *Lights, supra* note 49.

210 *Learning Styles, supra* note 173.

211 *Music, supra* note 15.

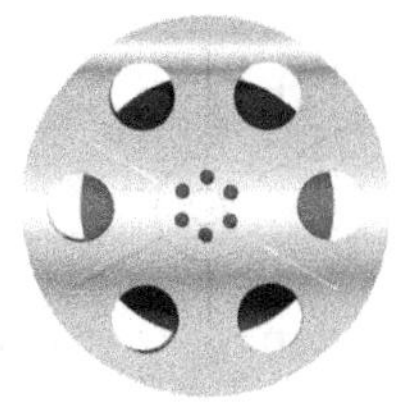

PROCESS DESIGN[212]

Similar to students who would enjoy Woman in Gold,[213] assimilators would appreciate Colonia[214] due to their aptitude to extrapolate concepts and apply them to present-day life scenarios. In this instance, students would apply the four steps in the creation of a truth and reconciliation commission and apply it to the outcome of the tragedy in Chile between the 1960s and 2004.

Pratt suggests that instructors who are concerned with social reform would use a film such as Colonia[215] to best demonstrate "critical examples of power and …how the selected group was impacted [and how] power differences are explored."

212 *Music, supra* note 15.

213 *Music, supra* note 15.

214 *Colonia, supra* note 16.

215 *Ibid.*

The film Colonia (2015),[216] starring Emma Watson,[217] was promoted as "a young woman's desperate search for her abducted boyfriend that draws her into the infamous Colonia Dignidad, a sect nobody has ever escaped from."[218] While Colonia[219] is promoted as a romantic, dramatic thriller, its fundamental intention is meant to draw attention to the horrific actions that took place in Chile between the 1960s and 2004. It is a largely an unknown piece of history that leaves ramifications still. As said in the documentary, Colonia Dignidad: A Nazi Sect in the Land of Pinochet (the documentary),[220] "This was a concentration camp in Latin America that lasted until 2004, and for some, it still exists today."[221]

After WWII, a former Nazi by the name of Paul Schäfer started a "private social mission"[222] for widows and orphans in Heide, Germany. The mission was supported by the German government from which Paul Schäfer and his partner, a Baptist priest, financially benefited. Years later, the mission and the building would be known as the location that founded the first Colonia Dignidad. As the years passed, rumours of Schäfer's homosexuality and paedophilia surfaced, as well as speculation that he was under investigation by a German crown prosecutor. Because of the pending investigation, Schäfer purchased fifty-five square miles in Chile, and he and three hundred of his followers journeyed there under the guise that they would be working with the Chilean people to help bring them out of poverty. The property purchased was termed "Colonia Dignidad" and is currently referred to as "Villa Bavaria."[223] In the 1970s, most thought the community was simply an organization with free schools, hospitals, medication, etc., supported by the government and utilized by local people. However, nothing had

---

216 *Colonia, supra* note 16.

217 Emma Watson, formally known for her role as Hermione Granger in the Harry Potter series, was cast to shed light on the atrocities that took place in Chile. It was determined that her fame would assist in this undertaking.

218 http://www.imdb.com/title/tt4005402

219 *Colonia, supra* note 16.

220 YouTube, "Colonia Dignidad a Nazi sect in the land of Pinochet" (January 2017) online: <www.YouTube.com/watch?v=5oObdFq78_s >. The author of this paper discovered the link ceased to be available through YouTube, as of date unknown, therefore a hyperlink is not possible.

221 *The Documentary, supra* note 242. At: 00h.50m.51s.

222 *The Documentary, supra* note 220.

223 Colonia Dignidad is now a German-themed holiday resort.

changed with Schäfer, and it soon became apparent that Colonia Dignidad was just another location to pursue his paedophilia and maintain his Jesus-like status.

During an interview for the documentary, Mrs. Muller,[224] a former settler, said this of Paul Schäfer:

> Mr. Schäfer came to see us in Austria in 1955; he came to my parents' home. That is where I first saw him and greeted him. When I looked at his face, I was overawed or startled. I thought I was seeing Jesus Christ.[225]

It was soon learned that the system he brought over from Germany was from the Hitler era, complete with gas and torture chambers. Subsequently, when other Nazi exiles heard of Schäfer, they got in touch with him, and Colonia Dignidad soon became a hideaway and a communications center central to the Nazi network in Latin America; this network was also known as "the Odessa Operation" and was aimed at helping Nazis relocate. It was said that Colonia Dignidad "provided Pinochet with services and skills acquired under Hitler."[226] After the coup in 1973 that gave the presidency to Pinochet, Schäfer offered its services to Pinochet and his new secret service, the National Intelligence Directorate or the DINA (with the intent to commit human rights violations). Soon, Colonia Dignidad became a political center of torture and missing persons.

Over the forty years that Colonia Dignidad was running, coverups were made by politicians, judges, businessmen, and police. In order to remove communist threats, underground bunkers with communication cables were set up to establish "Operation Condor," with the CIA providing the encoding equipment to do so. The CIA supported communication between Chile and Brazil, Argentina, Uruguay, and Paraguay through Operation Condor—and through their capitals and detention centers. That way, if someone was arrested in one of the countries, information could be sent through to the encoding equipment so that Chile could respond with the appropriate questions to ask the detained persons. Eventually, Colonia Dignidad housed a collection of semi-automatic guns, machine guns, and chemical weapons and was described as "a country within a country,"[227] with

---

224 Mrs. Gudrun Müller and her husband Wolfgang Müller left Colonia Dignidad in 2005.

225 *The Documentary, supra* note 220. At: 00h.02m.09s.

226 *The Documentary, supra* note 220. At: 00h.16m.08s.

227 *The Documentary, supra* note 220. At: 0h.34m.32s.

enough money—because of its profitable agriculture and businesses—to "buy another island."[228] Not long after, Schäfer left Chile for Argentina, where Interpol Argentina took the initial steps leading to his arrest in 2005.

As Hernán Fernández, a lawyer for child abuse victims, said in the documentary, "This is the only known case in the world where a system like this [was] set up to the sexual perversions, the paedophile, of the head of the organization, a kind of mass production to supply him with children."[229]

In 1990, after Pinochet's sixteen-year rule, President Patricio Aylwin immediately established the National Commission on Truth and Reconciliation Report,[230] which focused on Chile's history of human rights violations perpetrated by previous dictatorial leaders.

José Zalaquett[231] suggests that the report is in response to the "dilemma of our time,"[232] and may be summarized as follows:

> How can a country overcome a legacy of dictatorial rule and massive human rights violation if the new government is subject to significant institutional and political constraints? How, in those circumstances, can the equally necessary but often conflicting objectives of justice and social peace be harmonized? What are the moral tenets which should guide the politician's actions in such ambiguous situations?[233]

In creating the Truth and Reconciliation Commission and its subsequent report, Aylwin designed a process that meets the steps described in Designing Systems and Processes for Managing Disputes,[234] even though the report[235] was written twenty-three years earlier. Designing Systems[236] looks at four stages in process

228 *The Documentary, supra* note 220. At: 0h.47m.12s.

229 *The Documentary, supra* note 220. At: 00h.34m.00s.

230 Chile, Supreme Decree No. 355, Ministry of Justice, *Report of the Chilean National Commission on Truth and Reconciliation,* (Santiago: 25 April 1990).

231 José Zalaquet was a panel member of the Truth and Reconciliation Commission.

232 *The Report, supra* note 230 at 6.

233 *Ibid.*

234 Rogers, Nancy. Et al. Designing Systems and Processes for Managing Disputes (Frederick: Wolters Kluwer Law and Business (2013).

235 *Ibid.*

236 *Designing Systems, supra* note 234.

design: "1) taking design, initiative; 2) assessing or diagnosing the current situation; 3) creating systems and processes; and 4) implementation, evaluation and process of the design."[237] The first stage, deciding to become involved, took place on April 25, 1990, with Supreme Decree No. 355, and the creation of the Commission on Truth and Reconciliation. It considered nine elements, such as element number two, which addresses the need for justice and the creation of conditions to meet those needs. "That only upon a foundation of truth will it be possible to meet the basic demands of justice and create the necessary conditions for achieving true national reconciliation."[238] Included in the decree are nine articles.[239] The first article coincides with not only the approach to the report,[240] but also its first objective.[241]

> Article One:
>
> Let there be created a National Truth and Reconciliation
> Commission for the purpose of helping to clarify in a compre-
> hensive manner the truth about the most serious human rights
> violations committed in recent years in our country (and
> elsewhere if they were related to the Chilean government or to
> national political life), in order to help bring about the recon-
> ciliation of all Chileans, without, however, affecting any legal
> proceedings to which those events might give rise. Serious
> violations are here to be understood as situations of those
> persons who disappeared after arrest, who were executed, or
> who were tortured to death, in which the moral responsibility
> of the state is compromised as a result of actions by its agents
> or persons in its service, as well as kidnappings and attempts
> on the life of persons committed by private citizens for polit-
> ical purposes.[264]
>
> In order to carry out its assigned task, the Commission
> will seek:

237 *Ibid.*

238 *The Report, supra* note 230 at 24.

239 *The Report, supra* note 230 at 25.

240 *The Report, supra* note 230 at 28.

241 *The Report, supra* note 230 at 27.

1.   To establish as complete a picture as possible of those grave events, as well as their antecedents and circumstances;

2.   To gather evidence that may make it possible to identify the victims by name and determine their fate or whereabouts;

3.   To recommend such measures of reparation and reinstatement as it regards as just; and

4.   To recommend the legal and administrative measures which in its judgement should be adopted in order to prevent actions such as those mentioned in this article from being committed.[242]

In establishing the commission, Aylwin needed to gain acceptance of others in order to reach his directives. Contributing to the new human rights policy, other nations' policies were reviewed at the same time. They were watching Chile with great interest. Included in those observing were the United Nations and the Organization of American States[243]

Aylwin's administration was then ready to go to stage two, assessing or diagnosing the current situation. According to Designing Systems,[244] those who were "directly involved, affected by the conflict, or important to the success of a new design"[245] were sought out. Not surprisingly, the list of stakeholders involved in the report[246] is vast, and includes victims, their families, human rights organizations, national and international organizations, diplomats, and public and private agencies. The commission itself was made up of eight members, the staff, lawyers, law students, social workers, secretaries, technicians, and their assistants.

Once the team was organized, the commission needed to determine which cases would be considered. In addition, lists of those who died because of human rights violations were received from various organizations. These organizations included various military, political, and social groups, as well as "The Group of Relatives of those Arrested and Disappeared and the Group of Family Members

. . . .

242 *The Report, supra* note 230 at 25.

243 An organization meant to uphold the Charter of the United Nations.

244 *Designing Systems, supra* note 234.

245 *Designing Systems, supra* note 234 at 6.

246 *The Report, supra* note 230.

of those Executed Groups for Political Reasons, etc."[247] By establishing who would be involved, the commission was able to move to the next stage.[248]

Aylwin's third stage creates a design process and although it is simply stated, its meaning carries the weight of an entire nation, with the international community observing its outcome. Its monumental task is to design the methods of reparation of an entire nation.

Interestingly, the report[249] acknowledges and accepts the role the state has played and must play in restoration:

> Thus, we understand reparation to mean a series of actions that express acknowledgement and acceptance of the responsibility that falls to the state due to the actions and situations presented in this report. The task of reparation requires conscious and deliberate action on the part of the state.[250]

The report[251] notes the following main reparations: "Recommendations for restoring the good name of people and making symbolic reparation,"[252] "Legal and administrative recommendations,"[253] Recommendations in the area of social welfare,"[254] and finally, "The most urgent recommendations."[255] Each of these recommendations has a series of headings and sub-headings that break down each element. For example, "Recommendations for restoring the good name of people and making symbolic reparation"[256] focuses on the following: "Publicly repairing the dignity of the victims,""taking a position on the kind of gesture or creative expression that could best serve the proposed aims of restoring the good name of people and making reparation,"[257] and "solemnly restoring the good names

. . . .

247 *The Report, supra* note 230 at 30.

248 It is likely that stage one and stage two could be reversed.

249 *The Report, supra* note 230 at 1057.

250 *Ibid.*

251 *Ibid.*

252 *The Report, supra* note 230 at 1058.

253 *The Report, supra* note 230 at 1060.

254 *The Report, supra* note 230 at 1062.

255 *The Report, supra* note 230 at 1073.

256 *The Report, supra* note 230 at 1058.

257 *The Report, supra* note 230 at 1059.

of victims."[258]

The last few pages of this section acknowledge the need for more immediate measures to be addressed, and they include restoring the good name of the victims, declaring those who disappeared after they were arrested as dead so that the families can move forward, and, finally, establishing pensions for the families of the deceased.

Finally, Aylwin's fourth stage addresses the implementation of the system, and includes having tools in place should the reparation deteriorate. The report[259] is broken down into three sections, each one of those again into subsections. The first section is the introduction.[260] In the introduction, the report [261] reminds the reader that changes will not guarantee that human rights violations will not exist in the future, but that violations occur because of "an insufficient respect for those rights in a national culture. Hence we will have to include in our national culture the notion of unrestricted respect for, and adherence to, human rights and democratic rule." [262] The second section is "suggestions in the institutional and legal area to assure that human rights remain in force."[263] (Moreover, it addresses several factors or concepts: the re-alignment of a legal framework with international human rights law; that power-based operations, such as the police and the military, follow human rights obligations; improving national legislation; proper training of judges and lawyers; changing the constitution; plus creating an institution to protect human rights.) While this is only a brief overview of the section, it does provide a brief insight into the prevention of the violations. The third section, "suggestions aimed at consolidating a culture truly respectful of human rights,"[264] recommends that human rights should be part of the culture of everyday life and that each person should "internalize this principle so that behaviour in the home, schools and work, as well as in partisan political activity, in all exercise of authority, and very broadly in all activity, may be an application of that guiding principle."[265] It specifically targets and makes recommendations in two areas,

---

258 *The Report, supra* note 230 at 1060.

259 *The Report, supra* note 230 at 1075.

260 *The Report, supra* note 230 at 1057.

261 *The Report, supra* note 230 at 1075.

262 *The Report, supra* note 230 at 1076.

263 *The Report, supra* note 230 at 1077.

264 *The Report, supra* note 230 at 1104.

265 *Ibid.*

political activity and education, while still having society and the state embrace the new opportunity. Finally, the Aylwin administration looks at the fourth section: "truth, which must be "impartial, complete, and objective;"[266] justice, "which must be administered through the courts;"[267] and "reconciliation, as preventative measures."[268] The report[269] suggests those in a "position to help advance reconciliation with some gesture or specific act will do so."[270]

The United States Institute of Peace [271]suggested, as a follow-up to the report,[272] several measurable outcomes transpired because of the commission. First, that financial support continued for the families of the victims. Second, the report only addressed "victims of human rights violations outside of its mandate, including victims of torture that did not result in death or disappearance."[273] Finally, in 2009, the Chilean congress created a law that allowed for "re-opening the qualification of victims entitled to reparations."[274]

In closing, and perhaps most importantly, José Zalaquett eloquently addresses the impact of the report[275] on those who participated in its creation:

> Those who worked to produce the report became keenly aware of the cleaning power of truth. Interviewing thousands of relatives of victims and other witnesses nationwide was a necessarily rigorous method. But as the interviewers soon discovered, it was at the same time a means to heal the wounds, one by one, and thus to contribute to the building of lasting peace. They were also humbled by the generosity shown by the relatives of the victims they met. Certainly, many of them asked for justice.

266 *The Report, supra* note 230 at 1112.

267 *The Report, supra* note 230 at 1113.

268 *The Report, supra* note 230 at 1112.

269 *The Report, supra* note 230.

270 *The Report, supra* note 230 at 1113.

271 "Truth Commission: National Commission for Truth and Reconciliation (Comisión Nacional de Verdad y Reconciliación or the "Rettig Commission") 1 May 1990), Truth Commission: Chile 90, online: www.usip.org/ publications/1990/05/truth-commission-chile-90

272 *The Report, supra* note 230.

273 *Ibid.*

274 *Ibid.*

275 *The Report, supra* note 230.

Hardly anyone, however, showed a desire for vengeance.

Most of them stressed that in the end, what really mattered to them was to know the truth, that the memory of their loved ones would not be denigrated or forgotten, and that such terrible things would never happen again.[276]

Colonia[277] demonstrates a power-based process that devastated a country, leaving life-long scars on the victims and their families. Its purpose within the context of this paper is to introduce the assimilator-style student to a truth and reconciliation commission as an option in dispute resolution by comparing the report[278] to Designing Systems.[279] Pratt suggests that instructors who are concerned with social reform would use a film such as Colonia[280] to best demonstrate "critical examples of power and …how the selected group was impacted [and how] power differences are explored,"[281] and how truth and reconciliation commissions may be used to heal a nation.

276 *The Report, supra* note 230 at 17.

277 *Colonia, supra* note 16.

278 *The Report, supra* note 230

279 *Designing Systems, supra* note 234.

280 *Colonia, supra* note 16.

281 *Lights, supra,* note 30.

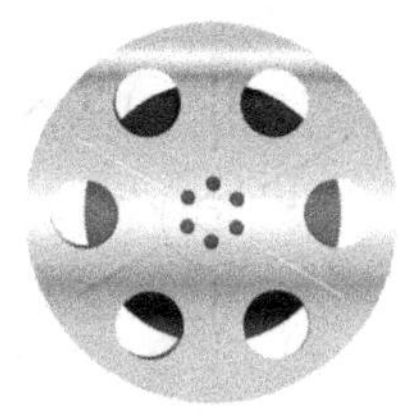

ADVANCED MEDIATION[282]

Attribution theory analyses the need to lay blame during a conflict scenario and, in War of the Roses,[283] attribution theory closely examines the breakdown of trust in the marriage between Barb and Oliver Rose. As in 12 Angry Men,[284] Pratt's accommodator style would appeal to students viewing War of the Roses,[285] as it would promote discussion around the analysis of attribution theory by providing concrete examples from the film. Furthermore, the teaching perspec-

282 *Advanced, supra* note 8.

283 *War, supra* note 17.

284 *Twelve, supra* note 11.

285 *War, supra* note 17.

tive that would best lend itself to this type of student would be the transmission perspective, as its style is meant to highlight content and address theoretical concepts.

In 1989, Danny DeVito directed War of the Roses,[286] a black comedy about the demise of a marriage. The audience is first introduced to the couple, Barbara Rose (Kathleen Turner) and Oliver Rose (Michael Douglas) five minutes into the film, on the last day of the tourist season in Nantucket. The camera angle is an aerial view overlooking the town. It is a rainy, gloomy, and overcast day, and while our first sound effect in the scene is one of light and happy music, full of hope and whimsy, it is actually playing second-fiddle to loud claps of thunder overhead. The audience sees Kathleen Turner running across the street to an estate auction, her suitcase over her head in an attempt to keep her dry. Michael Douglas is already at the auction, viewing items he is interested in purchasing. Each shot of the main characters is preceded by a clap of thunder, and we are, in literary terms, set up. As mentioned, the introductory music is full of hope and whimsy, and we are led to believe that something positive will happen to the main characters—they will meet, fall in love, and live happily ever after. After all, the music has led us to believe in fairy-tale endings. Unfortunately, not all is sunshine and daffodils, as claps of thunder increase in volume every time we are visually re-introduced to Oliver or Barbara. This literary device, called foreshadowing, tells the viewers that something is not quite right, and that this might not be the happy conclusion the storybook music foretells. But, for Oliver and Barbara Rose, and the audience, it was love at first sight. We buy into what the music offers—a happy ending—despite the fact the first word in the title of the film is war.

War of the Roses[287] beautifully addresses attribution theory, as Barbara and Oliver Rose blame the demise of their marriage on each other. As Graham and Folkes state in Attribution Theory: Applications to Achievement, Mental Health, and Interpersonal Conflict,[288] "Dissatisfied spouses tend to make more destructive causal attributions for their partner's conflict-related behaviour than do happy spouses."[289]

....

286 *Ibid.*

287 *War, supra* note 17.

288 Graham, Sandra. et al, Valerie S. Folkes, *Attribution Theory: Applications to Achievement, Mental Health, and Interpersonal Conflict* (Hillsdale: Lawrence Erlbaum Associates. Inc., Publishers 1990).

289 *Ibid, at 163.*

According to Gary Furlong's The Conflict Resolution Toolbox,[290] trust may be defined as "having positive expectations about another's motives and intentions toward us where potential risk is involved,"[291] and is a cornerstone of attribution theory. Furlong examines trust to be made-up of two key elements: risk, and motives and intentions. Risk is an analysis we take in achieving what we want, while motives and intentions are what we infer based on behaviours. Furlong explains when we assess someone's trustworthiness, we are assessing the other person's positive or negative intentions:

> If a risk is greater than the reward, the party is not likely to take
> the risk unless they have sufficiently positive expectations about
> the other party's motives and intentions; in other words, unless
> there is sufficient trust.[292]

Furlong's diagram, "Diagnosis with the Trust Model,"[293] describes three attributions. The first, "situational attribution," suggests there were factors outside the individual's control that led someone to behave the way they did, and little blame is placed on the other. This type of attribution is downplayed and often referred to as an oversight. Secondly, "intrinsic nature attribution" suggests the idea that the action is attributable to a person's nature and may be impacted by "culture, values, and past experience."[294] The final example is "intentional or hostile attribution," which places the blame entirely on the other party and suggests that the other party wishes to either cause harm or that they will gain something from causing harm.

290 Furlong, G. *The Conflict Resolution Toolbox* (Mississauga, ON: John Wiley & Sons Canada, Ltd., 2005).

291 *Toolbox, supra* note at 130.

292 *War, Supra* note 17.

293 *Toolbox, supra* note 290 at 132.

294 *Toolbox, supra* note 290 at 134.

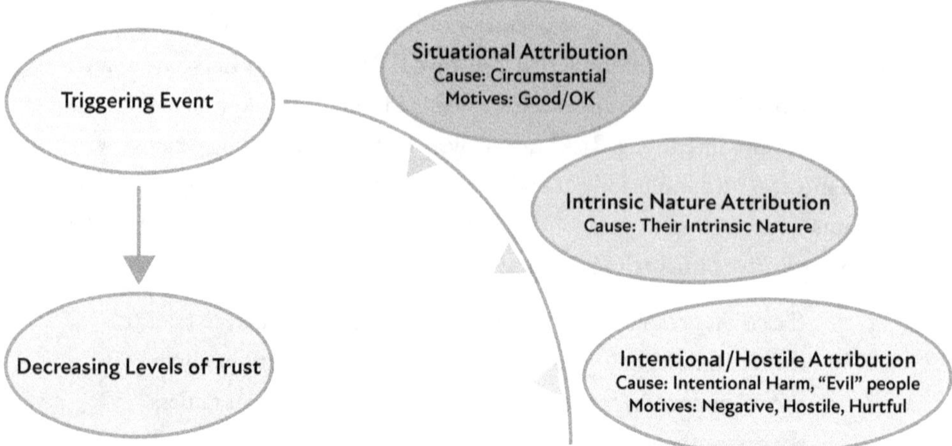

Furlong suggests that, as "motives and intentions cannot be seen, they can only be inferred from our interpretation of the other party's behaviour."[295] Moreover, Furlong suggests that an attribution is based on interpretation, either by assessing information or by preconceptions of "values, beliefs and past experiences,"[296] and that "seeing is not believing, but believing is seeing."[297]

In War of the Roses,[298] it is not clear when the triggering event took place or when the breakdown of the relationship began. However, at the beginning of their relationship, Barbara's view of Oliver would not rate high on the attribution scale (situational attribution); in fact, she blames most conflict on herself—such as when she places a tinfoil star at the top of the Christmas Tree early on in their marriage.

Barbara:	What do you think [of the star]?
Oliver:	It looks like tinfoil.
Barbara:	Oh, you're right, it doesn't make it. You are right, I'll learn.[299] Nevertheless, it is possible the first signs of the breakdown of the relationship began at a dinner party where Oliver tries to impress their dinner guests,

295 *Toolbox, supra* note 290 at 137.

296 *Ibid.*

297 *Ibid.*

298 *War, Supra* note 17.

299 *War, Supra* note 17. At 00h:12m:30s.

the partners at his law firm. This would be an example
of intrinsic attribution, as seen through the eyes
of Barbara:

Guest: Your crystal is lovely—it's not Waterford.
Oliver: Baccarat.

A hand thuds the table as the senior partner says, "Then we are paying our associates too much!"

There is a ridiculous laugh by Michael Douglas, and Kathleen Turner throws him a look in disgust.

In an awkward moment, Oliver asks Barbara to describe how they came to
purchase the Baccarat crystal: "Why don't you tell
it, Barb?[300]

Every guest at the table looks at her while she struggles to finish her food. Finally, she recounts the story: "We were in a lovely little place called 'The Pas de Cochon.'" Oliver corrects her: "Pied de Cuchon." She continues: "We were wondering around the Rue de Paradis …."[301] Oliver is seen at the other end of the table, mouthing: "Rue de Paradis," so she does not get the pronunciation wrong, and looks at his guests deciding whether they are enjoying Barbara's recollection of the story, or whether he should throw her a lifeline by finishing it off on her behalf. Knowing she would make a dog's breakfast out it, he steps in and saves the story, ultimately taking the focus away from his wife and bringing it back to himself. As he finishes the story, he tinkles the glass with his finger, and the camera moves to Barbara, who may be seen echoing the tinkle of his glass—except she uses her middle finger. This scene is particularly useful to the accommodator student, who would be able diagnose theoretical concepts of attribution theory by using Gary Furlong's "Trust Model."[302]

Both Julie Macfarlane, in Dispute Resolution Readings,[303] and Deutch and Coleman, in The Handbook of Conflict Resolution,[304] discuss Fritz Heider's

· ·

300 *War, Supra* note 17. At 00h:17m:22s.

301 *War, Supra* note 17. At 00h:17m:52s.

302 *Toolbox, supra* note 290 at 132.

303 *Dispute Resolution Readings, supra* note 40 at 33.

304 The Handbook of Conflict Resolution, Theory and Practice Michaela Keet,
     Coursepack: Handbook of Conflict Resolution, Theory and Practice (Faculty of Law,
     Osgoode Hall Law School, at York University, Summer 2016).

initial attribution theory, which suggests that people need to understand the causes of events around them so that they are able to make decisions about their own behaviour. It is suggested that behaviour is based on two elements: 1) disposition, such as personality traits, and 2) external circumstances. However, Jones, Davis, and Kelley extrapolate upon Heider's theory, and suggest that two stages must be met after one decides that the intentional act took place, because the "behaviour will produce the consequences observed (stage 1A) and the person has the ability to achieve the consequences [they] intend (stage 1B)."[305] Once it is established that the action was intentional, thoughts may turn to whether this is based on the person's disposition, stage 2:

The more the act has a strongly positive or negative effect on you, the more likely you are to attribute the behaviour to a corresponding disposition, stage 2A. Additionally, the more you perceive a positive or negative effect to be the intended result of the act, the more you attribute the behaviour to disposition, stage 2B.[306]

Jones, Davis, and Kelley suggest that in order to determine if an action is based on disposition or situational circumstance, three elements are reviewed:

A person behaves in the same way only under certain situations (distinctiveness information);

If the circumstances are consistent (consistency information); and

Where other people may act in a similar manner, given a similar situation (consensus information).

After the dinner party, we can see that Barbara attributed the unsuccessful evening to her husband, Oliver, and moved up Gary Furlong's "Trust Model"[307] from situational attribution to intrinsic attribution.

Oliver:	Well, I think everybody had a great time, don't you?
Barbara:	To make a long story short, no.
Oliver:	I'm sorry, you were just rambling on.
Barbara:	Well then, tell your own story next time. You care so desperately what everybody thinks, fuck-face!
Oliver:	They're my bosses!
Barbara:	They're Gavin's bosses, too. It didn't stop him from getting a foot-job all through dinner!

305 *Ibid* at 4.

306 *Ibid*.

307 *Toolbox, supra* note 290 at 132.

60

Oliver:	Gavin doesn't care about making partner; he doesn't have a wife and kids. I do. You want to keep living in this apartment? Because you do not buy a house on an associate's salary …at least not the kind of house that we want. OK, I care what they think. I care, all right? I care! Shoot me.
Barbara:	And that phony laugh. Hey heh heh heh.
Oliver:	That was a genuine laugh.
Barbara:	Hey heh heh heh.
Oliver:	OK, all right, all right. Maybe I overdid it. I was just trying to keep things going. God, I hope they didn't notice what a jerk I am.
Barbara:	They never seemed to.[308]

From this, we gather that Oliver doesn't typically act in such a peculiar manner, but was acting differently due to his bosses having dinner at their home (low consensus). We could assume that Barbara tends to attribute Oliver's behaviour to something internal to him.

However, if she recognized that he only acts like this around his bosses (high distinctiveness), is generally not so uncomfortable (low consistency), and that other people could act similarly if their bosses were over for dinner, Barbara could attribute his behaviour to external circumstances.[309]

Further study by Heider suggests that emotion plays a great deal into attribution theory, and that emotion could be impacted by either: 1) lack of effort of one party to change their own circumstances, which tends to evoke anger, or 2) the inability to change their own circumstances, which tends to evoke sympathy. Furthermore:

> Anger, resulting from a controllable attribution for another person's negative behaviour—whether it negatively affects oneself or other people—has been linked with punishing behaviour in general …. The anger that results from attributing such behaviour to a controllable cause arouses specifically retaliatory impulses, impulses to harm the other person.[310]

308 *Toolbox, supra* note 313 at 132.

309 *Handbook, supra* note 304 at 6.

310 *Handbook, supra* note 304 at 8.

This is referred to as the "attribution-to-emotion-to behaviour sequence,"[311] where first a judgement is made about the harmful behaviour of the other and if that behaviour was due to a reason beyond their control. As the audience realizes that Oliver and Barbara are basing their attributions on a misconception, harking back to Gary Furlong, who suggests that an attribution is based on interpretation, the result that becomes all too apparent in the film is the destructive nature of both parties leaves them unable to address their conflict at all. Since further study suggests we tend to attribute our own behaviour to situations beyond our control and that the other party has caused more harm than we have, Barbara and Oliver fall victim to this, as their loathing for each other increases with their destructive behaviour and they fall prey to accuser bias (the suggestion that the other person's action is under their own control, thereby impacting the other party in a negative manner).[312] This also leads to retaliation, as demonstrated throughout War of the Roses.[313]

Similar in concept and look to the Thomas Kilmann Model of Approaches to Conflict,[314] both Barbara and Oliver find themselves on the following figure, 11.2, as discussed in The Handbook of Conflict Resolution.[315]

The quadrants in the model below discuss the relationship between the level of responsibility between the "harmdoer's judgment of [their] own responsibility for harmful behaviour and the harmed party's judgment of [the] harmdoer's responsibility for harmful behaviour."[316] For example, if in quadrant one, both Oliver and Barbara agree that the harm was situational, then both parties could excuse the action. If in quadrant two, either Oliver or Barbara agree that the incident caused harm, one might apologize to the other, make amends, and move on. If in quadrant three, the harmdoer feels more responsible than the harmed, they might still be able to move forward with an apology or something similar from the harmdoer, which the harmed might believe is unnecessary. Finally in quadrant four, the harmed might demand that the harmdoer "make amends or face retaliation."[317] Ultimately, the difference in the

---

311 *Handbook, supra* note 304 at 9.

312 *Handbook, supra* note 304 at 10.

313 *War, supra* note 17.

314 Thomas, Kenneth W., Ralph H. Kilmann: "The Five Conflict-Handling Modes", online: <https://www.cpp.com/pdfs/smp248248.pdf>.

315 *Handbook, supra* note 304 at 11.

316 *Ibid.*

317 *Handbook, supra* note 304 at 1.

62

perceived responsibility could result in escalating anger for both parties, with dangerous results, as seen in War of the Roses.[318]

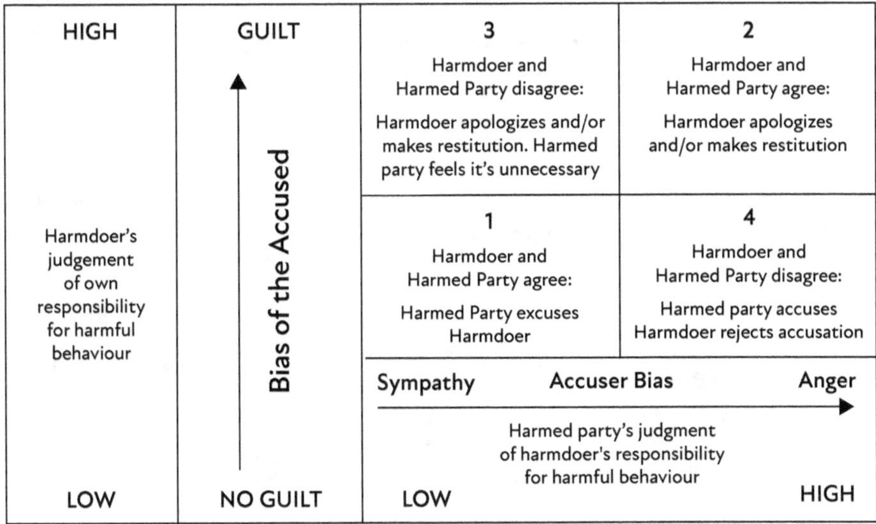

Figure 11.2 Combinations of Harmdoer's and Harmed Party's Judgments of Responsibility[319]

This escalating anger is depicted in the following diagram, referred to as the "Self-Perpetuating Cycle of Angry Conflict."[320] The diagram validates that unhappy couples attribute the other person's negative behaviour to controllable causes and positive behaviour to uncontrollable causes. In War of the Roses,[321] Barbara and Oliver Rose continue to perform in a negative manner towards each other based on the belief that it is retaliation for the negative behaviour of the other's performance toward them. In other words, the cycle of "payback" continues indefinitely, or until there is a conclusion to the situation. In many cases, the conclusion is divorce. In War of the Roses,[322] the introductory thunderstorm during the opening few minutes makes it easy for the audience, as it foreshadows the end of their relationship.

318 *War, supra* note 17.

319 *Handbook, supra* note 304 at 11.

320 *Handbook, supra* note 304 at 13.

321 *War, supra* note 17.

322 *Handbook, supra* note 304 at 11.

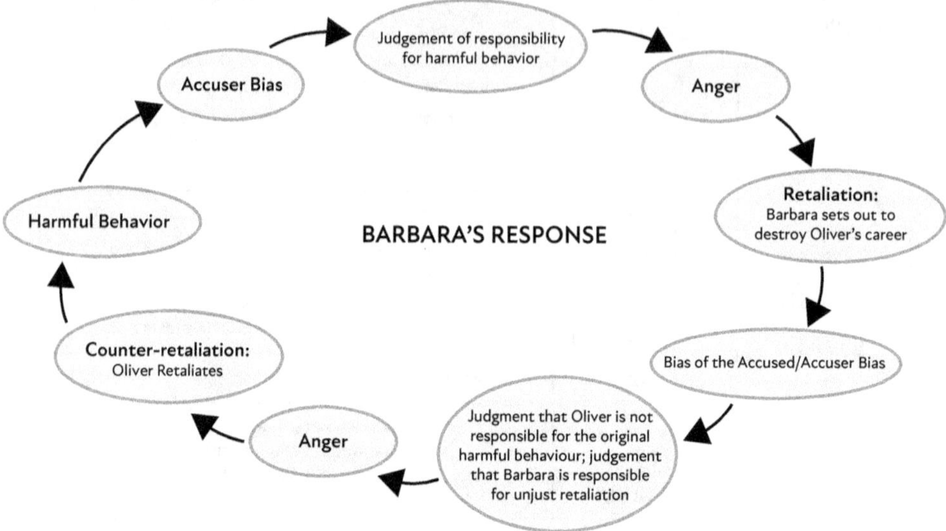

In a pensive moment, Gavin D'Amato (Danny DeVito) says of Barbara: "She laboured seven days a week to create the perfect home that Oliver always dreamed of. Not easy for a girl who grew up drinking her milk from glasses with chipped yellow flowers."[323]

Finally, we see Oliver move onto intrinsic attribution. While driving her Jeep, Barbara deliberately rolls his prized car (a previous Christmas present from Barbara to him), only with him inside the car. As he drags himself out of the car, he can be heard yelling as Barbara drives off: "OK, the gloves are off! Look, I don't want to create a scene, I live in this neighbourhood, too. BUT THE GLOVES ARE OFF!"[324]

Toward the conclusion of the film, an eery version of "Only you, can make my dreams come true…"[325] plays as Barbara pushes Oliver down their main staircase. We see a shot of a grandfather clock ticking and their chandelier swinging gently overhead. Both the clock and the chandelier foreshadow not only that time is

---

323 *War, supra* note 17. At 00h:23m:44s.

324 *War, supra* note 17. At 01h:32m:37s.

325 YouTube, "The Platters - Only You (And You Alone)" (5 March 2017), online: YouTube <https://www.youtube.com/watch?v=3FygIKsnkCw>

running out, but here is how it is going to happen.

Unfortunately, the Roses' relationship has run its course, with both parties moving from situational attribution to intentional attribution, both believing in their own way that they are less to blame than the other and that the only restitution from the other would be their demise. It is clear that neither Barbara nor Oliver will be happy until they have reached their objectives. In the final moments of the film, both of them have found themselves swinging from the great chandelier in the hallway; however, the chandelier is unable to sustain both their weights and it comes crashing to the ground. In a final act of reconciliation, Oliver moves his hand towards Barbara's as they both lay dying on the marble floor of the grand hallway, and in her last significant gesture, Barbara pulls her hand away. War of the Roses[326] appeals to Kolb's accommodator style as a learner and an apprentice perspective as an instructor, as it promotes discussion around theory and allows the student to analyze the theory and understand its importance in conflict situations. Films such as this have influenced the pedagogy of mediation by reviewing attribution theory by way of a black comedy.

326 *War, supra* note 17.

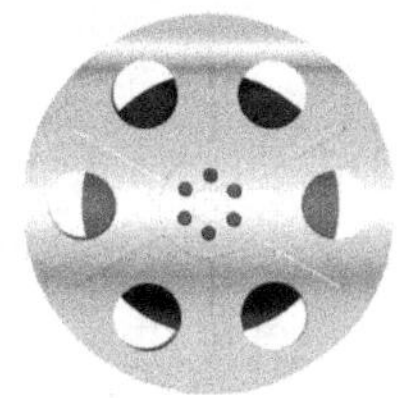

CULTURE, DIVERSITY, AND POWER[327]

In 2008, Clint Eastwood directed Gran Torino,[328] a challenging film that addresses the cultural clash between the cantankerous, foul-mouthed Korean War veteran, Walt Kowalski (played by Clint Eastwood), and his Hmong[329] neighbours, the Lors. "It demonstrates the differences between individualism and collectivism and high-context and low-context communication, as well the impor-

327 *Culture, supra* note 9.

328 *Ibid.*

329 Hmong are hill people from Laos, Vietnam, and Thailand and pre-date the Chinese. In 1997, they were recognized by the US government for helping them during the Vietnam War. The first influx of Hmong to the United States (and other countries including Canada) was 1975-1978.

tance of Stella Ting Toomey's "Face Negotiation Theory" (FNT) (Lightstone)."[330] This film would appeal to the divergent learner, as "they are able to look at things from a different perspective, and have broad cultural interests. They are interested in people [and] tend to be imaginative and emotional."[331] In addition, the developmental style of teaching perspectives "provides a case example for students to bridge their current knowledge to the new learning concepts."[332] This is important in Gran Torino,[333] as new cultural perspectives are introduced that might be unknown to the students—for example, individualism and collectivism, high and low-context culture, as well as the importance of face. Individualism may be defined as: "Cultures that value the individual over the group and tend to prize such qualities as independence, creativity, freedom of expression, and authority in decision making."[334] Collectivism refers to:

> The belief that the in-group is an end in itself, and that in-group members behave in ways that meet in-group expectations, not because of what they stand to gain as individuals, but because it is the right thing to do. An in-group is defined as a group whose norms, goals and values shape the behaviour of its members.[335]

High-context and low-context conversation patterns impact individualistic and collectivistic cultures differently. In a high-context culture, much of what needs to be said is implied, yet things not said are just as important as things that are said. It is expected that things that are unsaid are understood. Collectivistic cultures such as the Hmong are typically high-context cultures. In a low-context culture, such as some communities in North America, most of the communication is said with little room for an underlying context.

"Stella Ting-Toomey's Face Negotiation Theory (FNT) is a theory to aid in understanding how different cultures respond to conflict based on the concept

330 Helen Lightstone, "Confucius" (2016) 19.

331 *Lights, supra,* note 30.

332 *Ibid.*

333 *Gran, supra* note 19.

334 Ewert, C. et al, *Choices in Approaching Conflict: Understanding the Practice of Alternative Dispute Resolution* (Toronto, ON: Emond Montgomery Publications Limited, 2010).

335 *Lightstone, supra* note 330.

of face. The theory considers individualist and collectivistic approaches, as well as high and low-context concepts."[336]

As with all films, the content is often multi-layered, using elements to draw attention to the main character through an intricate storyline. Gran Torino[337] is also a bildungsroman,[338] a story whereby Walt Kowalski matures emotionally, psychologically, and spiritually with the help of people he never wanted or thought he needed to care for. This cinematic journey begins with his wife's funeral, with Walt standing alone at the altar, growling as each person enters the church. The audience is introduced to a lonely, solitary man, unhappy with his family, anchored emotionally to his time in the Korean War and his firm ethnocentric belief that the American way of life is the only way of life. Within the first few minutes of the film, we learn that his family wants as little to do with him as he does with them:

Son One:	Look at the old man, how he glared at Ashley. He can't even tone it down for Mom's funeral.
Son Two:	What do you expect? Dad's still living in the fifties. He expects his granddaughter to dress a little more modestly.
Son One:	Well, your kid's wearing a Lions jersey. I'm sure Dad appreciates that.
Son Two:	The point is that there's nothing anyone can do that won't disappoint the old man. It's inevitable. You know, that's why we stopped doing Thanksgivings ….
Son One:	What are we gonna do with him? Don't you think he's gonna get in trouble, all by himself in the old neighbourhood?
Son Two:	Well, why don't you have him move in with you?
Both chuckle.	
Son One:	Ha, ha, ha.[339]

Later in the day, as his wife's wake is ending, the Hmong family next door is happily celebrating the birth of a child with the traditional slaughter of a

336 *Ibid*

337 *Gran, supra* note 19.

338 The author bases the plot on the growth and development of the main character.

339 *Gran, supra* note 19. At 00h:02m:41s.

chicken.[340] The house is full of guests, and there is much activity surrounding the ritual conducted by the shaman. Walt mutters under his breath: "Damn barbarians."[341]

In contrast to the celebrations next door, Walt Kowalski is left alone in his home, and mumbles: "What the hell did chinks have to move into this neighborhood for?" [342]

The Hmong grandmother is also not without her own ethnocentric beliefs, and addresses Kowalski in Hmong, and in a manner equally as offensive: "Why does that old white man stay here? All the Americans have moved out of this neighbourhood. Why haven't you gone? Why don't you strut away, you dumb rooster?"[343]

Within the first twelve minutes of the film, we are introduced to two different cultures: the individualistic, low-context (characterized by Walt Kowalski) and the collectivistic, high-context (embodied by the Lors).

Throughout the film, Walt maintains a solitary, individualistic, low-context existence, choosing to live life the way he wants with as little interaction as possible from anyone, including the church or his family. After his wife's wake, he suggests the only reason anyone attended the luncheon after the service was that there was lots of ham, and takes himself to his garage to be alone. When his son and daughter-in-law visit, with the suggestion he move to a senior's home, he tosses them out of his house, throwing the gifts they brought for him out the door with them. In several instances, he may be seen watching television or sitting on his front porch with his only companion by his side, his dog, Daisy. If there is any communication, it is usually a growl or a swear word to scare someone into leaving. Resolute in making his own decisions, even death will be on his own terms. These examples are typical of someone from an individualistic culture.

According to Stella Ting-Toomey's FNT, Walt "would tend to express a greater degree of self-face maintenance in a conflict situation"[344] and "tend to use more dominating conflict styles,"[345] such as competing. This competing style is

. . . .

340 This is a traditional Hmong ritual at special events.

341 *Gran, supra* note 19. At 00h:10m:02s.

342 *Gran, supra* note 19. At 00h:11m:51s.

343 *Gran, supra* note 19. At 00h:11m:57s.

344 *Lightstone, supra* note 330 at 19.

345 *Ibid.*

demonstrated many times in the film with his use of weapons[346] to fend off the Hmong gang anxious to recruit Thao or to send a message to Thao's family.

> Walt: Ever notice how you come across somebody once in a while that you shouldn't have fucked with?[347]

Walt's approach to face is "self-face maintenance (the concern for one's own image), and is associated with a [contending] conflict management style."[348] Walt also demonstrates his low-context communication style to Father Janovich with wordy sentences showing his displeasure with the Father and the church: "Look, I appreciate the kindness you've shown to my wife. Now that you've spoken your piece, why don't you go tend to some of your other sheep? OK?"[349] and "Well, I confess that I never really cared for church very much. The only reason I went was because of her. And I confess that I have no desire to confess to a boy that's just out of the seminary."[350]

Unlike Walt Kowalski's individualist and low-context communication style, the Hmong family live in a high-context, collectivistic household. The first example of this is that the Lor family live in a multigenerational home, with grandparent, daughter, and two grandchildren sharing the same residence. Celebrations are always large family gatherings, in contrast to Walt, who begins his birthday celebrations sitting on the front porch with Daisy, drinking beer and eating beef jerky. There are very few scenes in the film where Thao's entire family are not present; even when a local Hmong gang try to recruit Thao, Thao's entire family run out to the front lawn, when Walt frightens the gang off the property. In another instance, Thao is brought to Walt Kowalski by his mother and sister to insist that Thao make amends to Walt for trying to steal his Gran Torino. Embarrassed by his own behaviour, Thao refuses to look Walt in the eye.

There are many instances where lack of eye contact is demonstrated—for example, no one looks at the shaman as he blesses a newborn.

While at Thao's house, Walt asks Sue, Thao's sister, "Hey, what am I doing wrong? Every time I look at somebody, they look at the ground." Sue replies, "Yeah, and a lot of Hmong people consider looking someone in the eye to be very

346 Weapons may be just the use of his hand pointed as a gun.

347 *Gran, supra* note 19. At 00h:34m:28s.

348 *Lightstone, supra* note 330 at 22.

349 *Gran, supra* note 19. At 00h:08m:02s.

350 *Gran, supra* note 19. At 00h:08m:22s.

rude—that's why they look away when you look at them."[351]

This is representative of Stella Ting Toomey's passive other-face, and demonstrates more accommodating-compromising and avoidance-oriented conflict strategies than members of individualistic cultures.[352] Collectivistic cultures tend to use more avoidance-oriented and compromising conflict strategies than individualistic cultures.

Walt Kowalski's trajectory from an individualistic reality to a collectivistic one ironically begins when his young neighbour Thao is coerced into stealing his 1972 Gran Torino. This action begins a series of events that tie the two families together. On Walt's birthday, Sue invites him to a family barbecue, where Walt is the guest of honour. Sue escorts him around the house, fixing food for him and explaining about their culture. He responds:

Walt:	Well, sounds dumb, but fine.
Sue:	Yeah, and a lot of Hmong people consider looking someone in the eye to be very rude—that's why they look away when you look at them.
Walt:	Anything else?
Sue:	Yeah, some Hmong people tend to smile or grin when they're yelled at. It's a cultural thing. It expresses embarrassment or insecurity, it's not that they're laughing at you or anything.
Walt:	Yeah. God, you people are nuts. But the food does look good. Smells good, too.[353]

After being "read" by the family shaman, he says to himself: "God, I've got more in common with these gooks than I do my own spoilt-rotten family."[354]

The next scene depicts Walt enjoying not only the food, but the women who are serving him.

Walt:	"Fantastic, you ladies are wonderful, this stuff is really good!"[355]

351 *Gran, supra* note 19. At 00h:44m:45s.

352 *Lightstone, supra* note 330 at 20.

353 *Gran, supra* note 19. At 00h:45m:05s.

354 *Gran, supra* note 19. At 00h:48m:10s.

355 *Gran, supra* note 19. At 00h:44m:44s.

As he is enjoying his meal, Sue says it is time to mingle, and reminds him that earlier he had asked her not to leave him alone. This scene demonstrates how Walt is being embraced by the collectivistic neighbours, and how he chooses to accept them.

Other collectivistic communities also appear in the film that create a challenge for Walt, For example, the gang communities may also be seen as a collectivistic group that maintain similar attributes. "For example, collectivistic cultures learn the major values of their group, such as harmony and cohesion, individuals tend to belong to in-groups that look after them in exchange for loyalty."[356]

In addition, the church is a collectivistic society that Walt wants little to do with, despite the persistent efforts of its priest, Father Janovich, demonstrated by the following quotes:

Father:	…your wife and I became quite close these last few months. She asked that I watch over you when she passed on.[357]
…	
Father:	Dorothy mentioned specifically that it was her desire for you to go to confession. She said she couldn't remember the last time you went.[358]
Walt:	Is that so?
Father	It is.
Walt:	Well, I confess that I never really cared for church very much. The only reason I went was because of her. And I confess that I have no desire to confess to a boy that's just out of the seminary.[359]
…	
Walt:	What are you peddling today, Padre?
Father:	Nothing. I thought I'd drop by and see you. I haven't seen you in church.

---

356 William E. Gudykunst, et. al, *"The Influence of Cultural Individualism-Collectivism, Self Construals, and Individual Values on Communication Styles Across Cultures."* (June 1996), online: <http://onlinelibrary.wiley.com/ doi/10.1111/j.1468-2958.1996.tb00377.x/full >

357 *Gran, supra* note 19. At 00h:07m:51s.

358 *Gran, supra* note 19. At 00h:08m:10s

359 *Gran, supra* note 19. At 00h:08m:22s.

Walt:	Now that you've done your good deed, why don't you take off down the road?
Father:	I'd really like to talk, Mr. Kowalski.
Walt:	Not in this lifetime, sonny.
Father:	Why? Do you have a problem with me, Mr. Kowalski?
Walt:	Well, I think you're an over-educated twenty-seven-year-old virgin who likes to hold hands of ladies who are superstitious and promises them eternity.[360]

Walt promptly slams the door.

Throughout this film, a very subtle choice of words tells the audience that Walt is beginning to accept the church. This can be heard when he first addresses Father Janovich. His term is a decidedly military reference, that of "Padre." Yet toward the end of the film, Walt begins referring to him as Father Janovich.

Sadly, facing his final showdown and accepting the church fully, he says under his breath: "Hail Mary, full of grace,"[361] as he is shot to save the Hmong family and help put the Hmong gang in prison.

Along the path of self-growth, Walt Kowalski takes a paternal role to Thao, assisting him in getting a job, to taking on a more patriarchal role as head of the Lors' house. In a patriarchal society, this is a much-respected role that Thao, living amongst the female members of his household, has not yet attained.

Grandma:	I want my daughter to find another husband. If she married again, there would be a man in the house.
Relative (in Hmong):	What about Thao? The man of the house is right there.
Grandma:	Look at him washing dishes—he does whatever his sister orders him to do. How could he ever become the man of the house?
Relative:	Be patient. Once he's older, he will be the man of the house.
Grandma:	No way.[362]

---

360 *Gran, supra* note 19. At 00h:12m:55s.

361 *Gran, supra* note 19. At 01h:40m:22s.

362 Gran, *supra* note 19. At 00h:10m:20s.

Gran Torino[363] addresses the importance of Stella Ting Toomey's Face Negotiation Theory and demonstrates the differences between a collective, low-context and an individualist, high-context culture. By playing Walt Kowalski off his Hmong neighbours, we see Walt Kowalski's bad-tempered attitude change throughout the film as he learns to understand and appreciate his new friends—so much so that he leaves his Gran Torino to Thao on the condition that he doesn't

> …chop-top the roof like one of those beaners, [doesn't] paint
> any idiotic flames on it like some white-trash hillbilly, and
> [doesn't] put a big, gay spoiler on the rear end like you see on
> all the other zipperheads' cars. It just looks like hell.[364]

This film would appeal to the divergent learner, as "they are interested in people [and] tend to be imaginative and emotional."[365] In addition, the developmental style of teaching perspectives "provides a case example for students to bridge their current knowledge to the new learning concepts."[366] Gran Torino[367] is an important learning tool, as new cultural perspectives such as individualism and collectivism, high- and low-context culture, as well as the importance of face are introduced to students who might be unfamiliar with different cultural perspectives on conflict and how it might impact disputes.

---

363 Gran, supra note 19.

364 *Gran, supra* note 19. At 01h:50m:17s.

365 *Lights, supra,* note 30.

366 *Ibid.*

367 *Gran, supra* note 19.

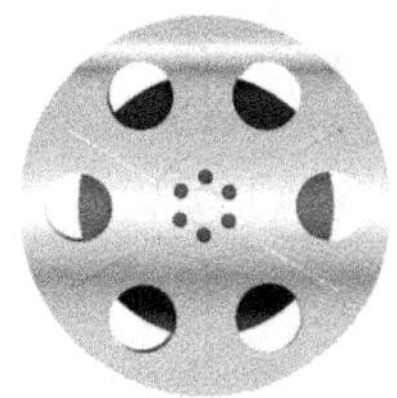

CONCLUSION

The purpose of this major research paper was to question whether film contributed to the pedagogy of dispute resolution by closely examining seven films. It provided a logical flow, following the LL.M. (DR) at Osgoode at York University and included, in chronological order: 1) Introduction to Dispute Resolution;[368] 2) Theory and Practice of Dispute Resolution;[369] 3) Process Design;[370] 4) Advanced Mediation;[371] and 5) Culture, Diversity, and Power.[372] In addition to addressing visual learners as those who are best adapted to learn via film, the MRP addressed which learning style and which teaching style best appealed to each film.

---

368 *Introduction, supra* note 5.

369 *Theory, supra* note 6.

370 *Process, supra* note 7.

371 *Advanced, supra* note 8.

372 *Culture, supra* note 9.

The following films best demonstrated key components of the dispute resolution program and the learning and teaching style best associated with them. "Introduction to Dispute Resolution"[373] addressed a dependent, integrative, win-win negotiation in The Tenth Man[374] and focused on the visual/special style of learning and the transmission approach to delivering content.

373 *Introduction, supra* note 5.

374 *Tenth, supra* note 12.

² *Women, supra* note 13.

² *Introduction, supra* note 5.

12 Angry Men[375] analyzed mediation concepts such as positions and interests, as well as the neutral skill sets required by a potential mediator. Furthermore, it best appeals to the accommodating style of the learner and the apprentice teaching perspective.

375 *12, supra* note 11.

Woman in Gold[376] addressed a power-based dispute (namely, the impact of the Nazi regime in WWII), which ultimately resulted in a three a three-panel arbitration process. It also appeals to the assimilator style of learning and the social reform perspective of teaching. The three films also demonstrated interest, rights, and power-based disputes suggested in the "Appropriate the Dispute Resolution Continuum."[377]

376 *Women, supra* note 13.

377 *Introduction, supra* note 5.

The "Theory and Practice of Dispute Resolution" addresses restorative justice by looking at the biblical approach of shalom, and the less religious perspective that looks to meet the needs of the victim, the offender, the families of both, and the community. Also reviewed were the eight elements of the individual justice needs as seen through the eyes of the offenders, the families, and the community. The documentary Music from the Big House[378] focuses on the need for the offender to acknowledge the harm caused.[379] The student who would most benefit from this film would be the divergent student, by the nurturing instructor.

378 *Music, supra* note 15.

379 *Ibid.*

The film Colonia,[380] based on the true story of Colonia Dignidad and Paul Schäfer, inspired the Report of the Chilean National Commission on Truth and Reconciliation. The President, Patricio Aylwin, implemented a process in developing the report[381] that matched the process as depicted Process Design.[382] As the report[383] aimed at healing the country, this film would best address the social reform style of instruction and appeal to the student who is more of an assimilator.

380 *Colonia, supra* note 16.

381 *The Report, supra* note 230.

382 *Process, supra* note 7.

383 *The Report, supra* note 230.

"Advanced Mediation"[384] closely examines "Attribution Theory" in War of the Roses[385] by reviewing trust and its cornerstones, risk, motives, and intentions. This film would also appeal to the instructor whose perspective is that of transmission, and the student who would best be defined as the accommodator.

384 *Advanced, supra* note 8.

385 *War, Supra* note 17.

Lastly, Gran Torino[386] plunges into discussion around the lack of communication between cultures and focuses on the relationship between a high-context, collectivistic household, represented by a Hmong family, and a low-context, individualistic Korean War vet living alone. It also reviewed "Face Negotiation Theory," and best defines the "Culture, Diversity, and Power" course.[387] This film would appeal most to the divergent student and the developmental instructor.

---

386 *Gran, supra* note 19.

387 *Lebaron, supra* note 9.

It is interesting to note that with the growing appetite for social media and its subsequent technology, most students today could fall into a visual/spatial learner category. By using film in the classroom, it assists students in viewing the world in different ways, and "[is] a springboard for active learning."[388] In addition, film allows students to gain insight into experiences they have little knowledge of, and simultaneously allows the adult learner[389] to tie their previous life experiences with their current knowledge, all of which provides greater depth to the content being taught.

It is clear that providing film as an alternative delivery method of information is not only well-received by students but by faculty as well. It is because of these concepts that this MRP delved thoroughly into the use of film as a teaching tool, and why it is so important to the pedagogy of learning.

388 *Lights, supra* note 30.

389 More mature students who are considered to have different reasons for returning to an academic environment.

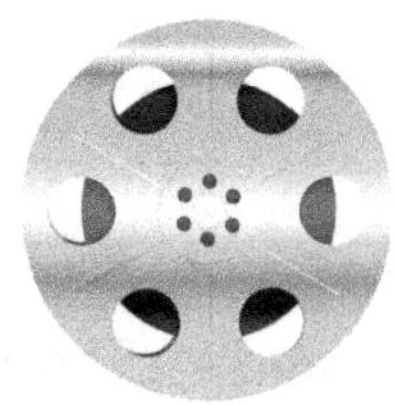

BIBLIOGRAPHY

LEGISLATION

Kunstrückgabegesetz ("Art Restitution Law"), BGBI. 1 Nr. 181/1998
Nichtigkeitsgesetz, ("Annulment Law"), BGBI. Nr. 106/1946

JURISPRUDENCE

Maria V. Altmann, Francis Gutmann, Trevor Mantle, and George Bentley, Dr. Nelly
Auersperg, v. the Republic of Austria (2006) (Arbitration, Vienna Austria)
(Arbitrators: Dr. Andreas Nödl, Lawyer Professor Walter H. Rechberger,
Professor Peter Rummel (Chairman).

GOVERMENT DOCUMENTS

Chile, Supreme Decree No. 355, Ministry of Justice, Report of the Chilean National
Commission on Truth and Reconciliation, (Santiago: 25 April 1990).

SECONDARY MATERIAL: ARTICLES

Helen Lightstone, "12 Angry Men: Themes, Conflict Theory and Mediators" (2016).
Helen Lightstone, "Confucius" (2016).
Helen Lightstone, "When Security is Ready" (2016).

SECONDARY MATERIAL: BOOKS

Bishop, P. et all, The Art and Practice of Mediation 2nd ed (Toronto, ON: Emond
Montgomery Publications Limited, 2015).
Ewert, C. et al, Choices in Approaching Conflict: Understanding the Practice of
Alternative Dispute Resolution (Toronto, ON: Emond Montgomery
Publications Limited, 2010).
Furlong, G. The Conflict Resolution Toolbox (Mississauga, ON: John Wiley & Sons
Canada, Ltd., 2005).
Graham, Sandra & Valerie S. Folkes, Attribution Theory: Applications to
Achievement, Mental Health, and Interpersonal Conflict (Hillsdale: Lawrence
Erlbaum Associates. Inc., Publishers 1990).
Lockhart, Art & Lynn Zammit, Restorative Justice: Transforming Society (Toronto,
ON: Inclusion Press, 2005).

Macfarlane, J. Dispute Resolution Readings, and Case Studies (Toronto, ON: Emond Montgomery Publications Limited, 2011).

Rogers, Nancy. et al. Designing Systems and Processes for Managing Disputes (Frederick: Wolters Kluwer Law and Business (2013).

Toews, Barb. The Little Book of Restorative Justice for People in Prison (Intercourse, PA, USA: Good BPPKS, (2006).

Zehr, Howard. Changing Lenses: A New Focus for Crime and Justice (Waterloo, ON: Herald Press, 2005).

SECONDARY SOURCES: COURSE CONTENT

D. Paul Emond, Adjunct Professor Leslie H. Macleod, Coursepack: Introduction to Dispute Resolution (Faculty of Law, Osgoode Hall Law School, at York University, Fall 2015) at 1.

Leslie H. Macleod, Coursepack: Dispute Analysis and Process Design (Faculty of Law, Osgoode Hall Law School, at York University, Winter 2016) at 1.

Leslie H. Macleod, Coursepack: The Theory and Practice of Dispute Resolution (Faculty of Law, Osgoode Hall Law School, at York University, Fall 2015) at 1.

Michaela Keet, Coursepack: Advanced Dispute Resolution (Faculty of Law, Osgoode Hall Law School, at York University, Summer 2016) at 1.

Michelle LeBaron, Coursepack: Culture Diversity and Power in Dispute Resolution (Faculty of Law, Osgoode Hall Law School, at York University, Spring 2016) at 1.

Mary Giardina, Coursepack: Teaching and Training Adults, Coursepack (Faculty of Seneca College Fall 2011) at 2.

INTERNET

"Annulment Act," (15 May 1946), online: <http://www.ris.bka.gv.at/Dokumente/BgblPdf/1946_106_0/1946_106_0.pdf>

"Arbitral Award", online: <https://www.unodc.org/res/cld/case-law- doc/traffickingculturalpropertycrimetype/aut/maria_altmann_vs republic_of_austria_html/A rbitral_Award_-_5_Klimt_paintings_Maria_V._Altmann_and_others_v._Republic_of_Austria-_15_January_2004.pdf. The author of this paper discovered the content ceased to be available, as of February 5th, 2023, therefore a hyperlink is not possible. https://mubi.com/notebook/posts/movie-poster-of-the-week-music-from-the-big-house.

Durham College, "Overview of 3 UDL Principles", online: <https://durhamcollege.ca/ctl/teaching/planning-to-teach/udl/3-udl-principles// https://www.usip.org/publications/1990/05/truth-commission-chile-90

KJV Unknown, "Exodus 18King James Version (KJV)" online: Exodus 18:https://www.biblegateway.com/passage/?search=Exodus%2B18&version=KJV.

"Restitution Act" (4 December 1998), online: http://www.ris.bka.gv.at/Dokumente/BgblPdf/1998_181_1/1998_181_1.pdf>.

Stewart, D. P. "The Foreign Sovereign Immunities Act: A Guide for Judges.

Georgetown University Law Center, Federal Judicial Center International Litigation Guide", online: https://wrlc-gulaw.primo.exlibrisgroup.com/discovery/fulldisplay?docid=alma9912765266204101&context=L&vid=01WRLC_GUNIVLAW:01WRLC_GUNIVLAW&search_scope=MyInst_and_CI&isFrbr=true&tab=Everything&lang=en

Thomas, Kenneth W., Ralph H. Kilmann: "The Five Conflict-Handling Modes", online: <https://www.cpp.com/pdfs/smp248248.pdf>.

Unknown, "David Kolb's Learning Styles Model and Experiential Learning Theory (ELT)" (March 2017) online: https://www.businessballs.com/self-awareness/kolbs-learning-styles/%23:~:text=Diverging (feeling and watching - CE, situations from several different viewpoints.

Unknown "Teaching with Film", Journeys in Film, online: https://journeysinfilm.org/articles/teaching-with-primary-sources-through-film/

Unknown, "litereary-devices.com/content/bildungsroman", online: https://literarydevices.com/bildungsroman/

Unknown, "The Organization of American States", online: http://www.oas.org/en/about/who_we_are.asp>.

Unknown, "Theory of Multiple Intelligences", online: <https://openoregon.pressbooks.pub/educationallearningtheories3rd/chapter/chapter-9-theory-of-multiple-intelligences-2/>

YouTube, "Colonia Dignidad a Nazi sect in the land of Pinochet" (January 2017) online: <www.YouTube.com/watch?v=5oObdFq78_s >. The author of this paper discovered the link ceased to be available through YouTube, as of date unknown, therefore a hyperlink is not possible.

YouTube, "The Platters - Only You (And You Alone)" (5 March 2017), online: YouTube https://www.youtube.com/watch?v=3FygIKsnkCw>

ONLINE JOURNALS

"Exodus 18King James Version (KJV)", online: Exodus 18:

"Truth Commission: National Commission for Truth and Reconciliation (Comisión Nacional de Verdad y Reconciliación or the "Rettig Commission") 1 May 1990), Truth Commission: Chile 90, online: https://www.usip.org/publications/1990/05/truth-commission-chile-90

Anne Laure Bandle, Sarah Theurich, "Alternative Dispute Resolution and Art-Law - a New Research Project of the Geneva Art-Law Centre", online: (2011) Retrieved from Journal of International Commercial Law and Technology: https://www.neliti.com/publications/28706/alternative-dispute-resolution-and-art-law-a-new-research-project-of-the-geneva.

Pamela Eddy, Daniel Bracken, "Lights, Camera, Action! The Role of Movies and Video in Classroom Learning", (2008) 22 Journal of Faculty Development 2 online: <

http://www.questia.com/library/journal/1P3-1619018211/lights-camera-action-the-role-of- movies-and-video>. The author of this paper discovered the website ceased to be available, as of December 21st, 2020, therefore a hyperlink is not possible.

Caroline Renold, Alessandro Chechi, Anne Laure Bandle, Marc-André Renold, "Case Six Klimt Paintings – Maria Altmann and Austria", online: (2012) Arthemis Art-Law Centre University of Geneva <https://plone.unige.ch/art-adr/cases-affaires/6-klimt-paintings-2013-maria-altmann-and-austria/case-note-2013-six-klimt-paintings-2013-maria-altmann-and-austria.
Constance Lowenthal, "Recovering Looted Jewish Cultural Property", online: (2004) 7:6 Permanent Court of Arbitration < https://pca-cpa.org/en/home/>.
Stephen J. Ware, "Arbitration and Assimilation", 7:4 Washington University Law Review online: (1999) https://journals.library.wustl.edu/lawreview/article/id/5933/
Washington Conference Principles on Nazi-Confiscated Art", online: Commission for Looted Art in Europe: https://www.lootedartcommission.com/home.
William E. Gudykunst, et. al, "The Influence of Cultural Individualism-Collectivism, Self Construals, and Individual Values on Communication Styles Across Cultures." (June 1996), online: <http://onlinelibrary.wiley.com/doi/10.1111/j.1468-2958.1996.tb00377.x/full >

CONFERENCES

Stuart E. Eizenstat, "In Support of Principles on Nazi-Confiscated Art: Holocaust-Era Assets" (Presentation) delivered at the Washington Conference, 3 December 1998).

FILM

12 Angry Men, DVD (Beverly Hills, Cal: Twentieth Century Fox Home Entertainment, 2008)
Burning Bridges, DVD (The International Institute for Restorative Practices, 2011).
Gran Torino, DVD (Warner Bros. Pictures, 2008).
Music from the Big House, DVD (Caché Film and Television, 2012)
The Tenth Man, DVD (Metro Goldwyn Mayer, 2005).

ONLINE FILM

Netflix, "Colonia" (November 2015). Online: Netflix <www.netflix.com/search?q=Colonia>
ITunes, "Woman in Gold" (December 2015). Online: iTunes</C:\Users\Owner\Music\iTunes\iTunesMedia\Movies\Woman in Gold\Woman in gold (HD).m4>
ITunes, "War of the Roses" (December 2016). Online: iTunes < C:\Users\Owner\Music\iTunes\iTunes Media\Movies\The War of the Roses\The War of the Roses (HD).m4>

COMPACT DISK

Rita Chiarelli, "Music from the Big House "Soundtrack," CD: I Love You Still.

(Louisiana State Prison, Toronto,
Mad Iris Music Inc. 2011).
Rita Chiarelli, "Music from the Big House "Soundtrack," CD: Glory. (Louisiana State
    Prison, Toronto,
Mad Iris Music Inc. 2011).
Rita Chiarelli, "Music from the Big House "Soundtrack," CD: These Four Wall.
    (Louisiana State Prison, Toronto,
Mad Iris Music Inc. 2011).

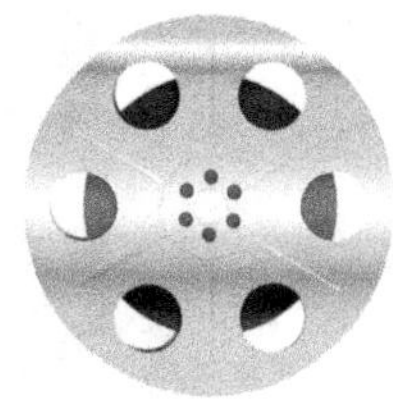

APPENDIX

The 10th Man.

One major customer of the Citroen U23, a light truck introduced in 1935, was the French military. At the time of the German invasion, more than twelve thousand had been delivered in less than ten months. About six thousand were pressed into German service after the French defeat of June 1940.

12 Angry Men.

In the early evening of May 12, 1955, a train pulled out of Lower Manhattan's Chatham Square, near City Hall, bound for upper Manhattan and the Bronx via Third Avenue. It was the last run of the Third Avenue elevated, and the last time a train ran up a large chunk of Manhattan east of Lexington Avenue for six decades.

Woman in Gold.

The Steyr 50 was a small car released by the Austrian automobile manufacturer Steyr-Daimler-Puch AG. It was regarded as the "Austrian Volkswagen" and was affectionately referred to as the "Steyr Baby."

Music from the Big House.

Long is the road from New Orleans to Angola, but it's a worn path—there being a near-constant stream of people making the trip. Many of the folks going, we know, are going involuntarily.

Colonia.

1970 saw the start of production for an unusual vehicle under President Salvador Allende in Chile. The Yagan stood for Chilean socialism's approach to technologies and the materialization of Allende's utopian project.

War of the Roses.

Morgan Plus 4 production ran from 1950 to 1969, and was revived in 1985 until 2000. In the film, Barbara Rose buys a 1960 Morgan Plus 4 for her husband Michael, then, after their marriage sours, destroys it by crushing it under her GMC Jimmy.

Gran Torino.

Walt Kowalski's prized possession in the film, the 1972 Ford Gran Torino, is a third-generation Ford Torino, with one of its most radical redesign elements being the egg-crate grill, likened to the mouth of a killer whale.

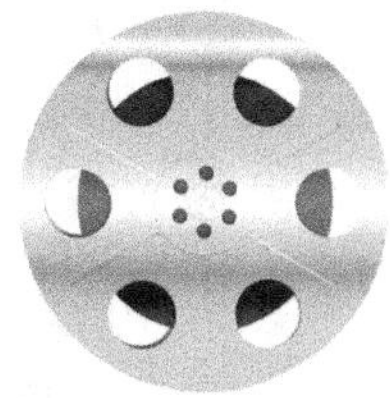

AUTHOR

Helen Lightstone, LL.M, is a chartered mediator and qualified arbitrator with more than seventeen years as a conflict resolution practitioner under her belt. Currently practicing in Ontario, Canada, Lightstone is considered an industry leader in conflict resolution training. She is a member of the Law Society of Ontario and the Alternative Dispute Resolution Institutes of both Ontario and Canada, and her company, Lightstone Academy for Conflict Resolution, offers two forty-hour courses, and one twenty-one-hour course, on alternative conflict resolution all accredited by the Alternative Dispute Resolution Institute of Ontario.

After years of building her incredibly successful career, Lightstone returned to school and received her Master of Laws from Osgoode Hall at York University in 2017. Inspired by her insights watching films like 12 Angry Men, she produced her major research paper with the hopes of exploring how film can be used to teach alternative dispute resolution. Recognizing it as a unique and underexplored pedagogical tool, she decided to share her expertise more broadly, publishing her paper as her first book. She hopes to help negotiators, mediators, arbitrators, and disputants themselves through her work.

Outside of her career interests, Lightstone also enjoys photography, travel, theatre, gardening, and kayaking. She lives in Whitby, Ontario with her two dogs—Cookie Pearl and her "long-retired" first dog, Esme. You can find her on her website, lightstoneacademy.ca, or on Twitter, Instagram, LinkedIn, or Facebook.

ILLUSTRATORS

Bronagh Morgan's favourite car is her bike, and favourite way to get around is her feet. A middle-distance runner, lawyer and future mediator (thanks Helen!), Bronagh is a Niagara Falls-born artist whose preferred media include pencil, pastel, charcoal, markers and kids' sidewalk chalk. This is her first book of illustrations. She'll probably bring her kids to pick up a few hundred copies in her beloved 2012 Ford Fiesta.

Keep up with her on Instagram @bronagh.joyce and Twitter @ThatBronaghOne

With a love of art spanning a lifetime Lori E. Felix is an illustrator, painter, and graphic artist. While largely self taught in fine arts and painting, Lori did attend the Graphic Design program at Durham College. When Lori isn't working in her studio you can usually find her spending time with her family or teaching karate at the local martial arts club.

Lori may be reached at Be a Part of the Art by Lori on Facebook or at beapartoftheartbylori@outlook.com